SpringerBriefs in Education

More information about this series at http://www.springer.com/series/8914

Mary Renck Jalongo · Crystal Machado

Making Effective Presentations at Professional Conferences

A Guide for Teachers, Graduate Students and Professors

Springer

Mary Renck Jalongo
Journal Editor
Springer
Indiana, PA
USA

Crystal Machado
Indiana University of Pennsylvania
Indiana, PA
USA

ISSN 2211-1921 ISSN 2211-193X (electronic)
SpringerBriefs in Education
ISBN 978-3-319-23173-0 ISBN 978-3-319-23174-7 (eBook)
DOI 10.1007/978-3-319-23174-7

Library of Congress Control Number: 2015951517

Springer Cham Heidelberg New York Dordrecht London

Printed on acid-free paper

Springer International Publishing AG Switzerland is part of Springer Science+Business Media
(www.springer.com)

Preface

There is no shortage of advice on making effective conference presentations; a Google search of that phrase yielded 432,000,000 results. However, much of this information is general rather than focused on the types of presentations made by teachers/scholars in Academia. Making effective presentations to fellow professionals at conferences is an important contribution for educators at all levels, from basic through higher education. This *SpringerBriefs in Education* prepares teachers, college students, and higher education faculty to conduct various types of presentations, including: (1) workshops and professional trainings, (2) poster sessions, (3) panel discussions, (4) roundtables, (5) research forums, and (6) technology-supported presentations. It takes the approach of a "paper mentor" that guides readers through the use of templates, specific examples, and a wide range of online resources.

Why This Monograph at This Time?

In reviewing the literature on making effective conference presentations, several areas were lacking.

1. Most other writings on this topic consist of a collection of tips for presenters rather than a review of the relevant literature; this monograph reviews the literature across disciplines to provide a wide array of authoritative resources for presenters.
2. No other books we found in our literature review included the full range of presentations possible at professional conferences. This SpringerBriefs includes conference session formats that were not discussed elsewhere, such as presenting from afar with technology support, planning a panel discussion, or preparing a research poster session.
3. Other books about making effective conference presentations did not speak to presenters at different levels of experience, from novice to expert.

This SpringerBriefs provides support to presenters from graduate students making their initial foray into conference presentations to tenured, full professors seeking to hone their craft as keynote speakers.

4. Other titles did not actually *teach* the reader how to accomplish important tasks; the proposed SpringerBriefs includes a wide array of helpful tools, examples, and templates to assist readers in planning, proposing, conducting, and evaluating conference presentations.
5. We conducted an extensive search of authoritative online sources about making conference presentations that are easily accessed and free of charge. Each chapter includes an annotated list of the most helpful online resources.

We approached writing this SpringerBriefs as an answer to two important questions: (1) What do we wish we had understood long ago, when we first started presenting at conferences? and (2) What book could simultaneously serve as a resource for the more experienced scholar? With these goals in mind, we have prepared a comprehensive and concise guide to many different types of conference presentations and guidance in developing strategies that support successful outcomes for teachers, scholars, and researchers.

Contents

Part I
Presenters and Their Audiences

Chapter 1
Making Presentations to Fellow Professionals: A Rationale

Making conference presentations is in some ways an outgrowth of effective teaching. For example, successful conference sessions depend on identifying appropriate objectives, preparing thoroughly, and evaluating the outcomes. In other ways, however, a conference presentation represents a task that is distinctive from teaching. Now the audience consists of adult peers rather than students over whom the presenter has some authority. As a result, conference participants generally feel freer to challenge the presenter or to exit the session in search of something better. Thus, making conference presentations requires educators to expand their teaching repertoires and acquire specialized skills related to the specific types of presentations that they seek to offer, ranging from a one-hour workshop/training to full day preconference institute. This chapter sets the stage for all of the remaining chapters by exploring the various forms of professional dialogue that are necessary to advance thinking in various fields. It begins by describing the role with which most readers will be thoroughly familiar: that of attending professional conferences. It then guides readers in understanding the principles of effective presentations by asking them to reflect on their best/worst experiences as a participant, thereby gaining insight into characteristics of effective and ineffective conference sessions. The chapter concludes by building the foundation for all successful presentations; namely, audience awareness. With this as a starting point, presenters can move beyond a preoccupation with self-as-presenter that will enable them to design effective conference presentations for various audiences and purposes.

On the Value of Conferences

As a first step in presenting at conferences, it is helpful to reflect on why professionals throughout the world participate in these events (Ernst 2004; Hay et al. 2005). Common goals of participation in conferences for scholars include:

- *Keeping up to date*. Possibly the most common reason for attending a conference is to keep current. There often is a time lag of nearly 2 years between acceptance of a journal article in a highly competitive outlet and its publication;

M.R. Jalongo and C. Machado, *Making Effective Presentations at Professional Conferences*, SpringerBriefs in Education,
DOI 10.1007/978-3-319-23174-7_1

an even longer time lapse frequently occurs between submitting a book proposal and the publication of a book. As a result, conference presentations frequently are more up-to-date than the professional literature currently in print.

- *Building expertise.* At large conferences, it is possible to select a particular theme or strand and follow it through the program in order to improve confidence and skill in a particular area. Novices gain experience as presenters and get valuable feedback on their research or learn about the latest methods, tools, and issues (Tappe and Galer-Unti 2009). Established scholars forge career-long relationships as they serve on committees together, identify a shared research interest, or decide to collaborate.
- *Advancing professionally.* For graduate students, getting on the conference program of a leading professional organization improves their chances of getting job interviews and offers of employment. For faculty members, a respectable showing of presentations at professional conferences plays an undeniable role in tenure and promotion. In addition, participation in conferences can provide information about employment and funding opportunities. Not all of the learning that takes place at a professional meeting occurs in formal sessions; many times, informal networking is equally important to professional advancement (Fischer 2006; Vega and Connell 2007). There are at least four professional benefits explained below.

Entering the Professional Dialogue

As Jerome Bruner (1996) has observed, the learning process typically relies on meaningful dialogue between the more experienced and the less experienced. Even the most prominent expert in the field may have less experience with particular aspects of a topic than members of the audience. To illustrate, a leading expert was making a presentation to teachers about working with children who have pervasive developmental disorders, such as autism. One of the audience members worked with an organization that provides specially trained service dogs to work with this population—something that the presenter did not know that much about but definitely wanted to understand better. When everyone is respectful of everyone else's specialized expertise, professional dialogue is supported. New presenters who worry that members of their audience are more knowledgeable and experienced than they are need to keep this in mind. There are many forms of expertise and they are distributed among the audience; no one is expected to know it all.

Creating a Professional Network

Without a doubt, the world of Academia can be fraught with pressures to be a productive scholar. Curriculum vitae cite all of the achievements but not the many failed attempts behind those successes. One source of support when scholars encounter the inevitable disappointments during a career is the establishment of a group of respected professionals outside the faculty member's home institution. No matter how supportive departmental colleagues are, the fact remains that they frequently serve as evaluators of fellow departmental colleagues. Given this evaluative function, new faculty members may be understandably reluctant to speak about their failures, seek advice, or confess to self-doubt. Colleagues outside the department or institution offer numerous advantages. First of all, they have no authority over the new faculty member's situation with an employer. Secondly, they often share a particular research interest with the new faculty member that colleagues in his or her home institution do not. Third, faculty members from other institutions have potential as collaborators on presentations, research, and publications. Finally, these faculty members from other institutions provide a respite from the inner workings of a particular academic department or perhaps, a fresh and impartial perspective that puts a persistent issue into perspective.

Documenting Scholarly Productivity

College and university faculty members are routinely required to document their scholarly productivity. Decisions about tenure, promotion, book contracts, awards, and other forms of professional recognition rely, to a considerable extent, on a respectable number of scholarly achievements. Although institutions vary widely in what "counts" as scholarship, presentations at the major conferences are an important way of demonstrating that faculty members have earned the respect of peers (Rébék-Nagy 2008). Many scholars find that, at first, they need to submit numerous conference proposals in order to get on the conference program. However, as they gain confidence and skills, nearly every proposal is accepted and they cannot afford the time and expense to present at so many conferences. This outcome should be interpreted as the time to become more selective about conferences and to take successful sessions to the next step of publication (see Chap. 11).

Mentoring Professional Colleagues

Graduate students and new faculty members frequently begin with less competitive conference presentations and "work their way up" to the more prestigious, peer-reviewed national and international meetings. For well-established scholars, conferences frequently are a way to mentor graduate students and less experienced colleagues. Figure 1.1 provides advice on mentoring first-time presenters.

1. *Plan the trip*. Share cell phone information, itineraries and all relevant hotel information (e.g., confirmation number, shuttle services). When making hotel reservations, try to reserve a block of rooms together.
2. *Offer advice on what to take*. Each presenter should carry a copy of all of the resources for the presentation, just in case someone cannot participate at the last minute. Do not assume that students already know what types of attire are appropriate for the event and advise them accordingly. If participants are inexperienced air travelers, refer them to the airline's website for rules and regulations.
3. *Review the conference program*. Discuss ways to select which presentations to attend. Novices at attending conferences sometimes select by topic alone, so recommend some dynamic speakers that are role models.
4. *Be considerate of financial constraints*. Costs should be discussed with the participants and their budgets ought to be respected when looking into transportation and meal options. Advise others of any travel support available at the university or through professional organizations.
5. *Make an agenda for everyone to follow*. Determine who will be responsible for each part of the presentation and how long each section will take. All presenter activities--including assembly and clean-up of presentation areas--should be planned.
6. *Rehearse as a group*. Conduct the "dress rehearsal" and actually time each contribution so that no one goes off on a tangent and cuts into another presenter's time. First-time presenters at a professional conference may feel more comfortable if they have practiced in front of a campus audience prior to the professional conference, so identify opportunities to do this.
7. *Check out the local arrangements*. After arriving at the conference, the group should investigate the room where the presentations will be made to feel better prepared and do an equipment check.
8. *Follow the group's agenda*. Remind everyone that you will serve as time keeper and give them a "two minute warning" with a subtle signal, such as making eye contact and nodding. Keep a watch on the podium and, when you introduce each person, remind him or her of the time allocation (e.g., Thank you, ___. For the next 10 minutes, ____ will explain the planning process for the project.)
9. *Reflect on the session*. Critique the session afterwards and plan for improvements. Look for opportunities to share what was learned at the conference with others (Adapted from McGuire, Simpson and Duke, 2009)

Fig. 1.1 Mentoring first-time presenters

Maximizing the Value of Conference Participation

When professionals first begin attending conferences, it often is with a "collecting" mentality. They attend as many sessions as possible in search of material that will be useful in their work, gather it up, and then discard what is not worth carrying home. More experienced conference attendees have learned how to maximize the value of their attendance at conferences by being more selective. If they attend the same conference regularly, they begin to know who can be depended upon to deliver a high-quality session and seek out those individuals. They also learn to exit the session if it becomes clear that the presenters are not well prepared or if it was not what they expected. In addition, savvy participants in professional conferences have learned to make the conference work for them by identifying experiences that will support a particular professional goal. Suppose, for example, that a graduate student or professor has the goal of becoming more involved in publishing research.

Before the Conference

- make a plan for keeping everything running smoothly at home and at work while you are away
- create a "to do" checklist so that you don't forget anything important, such as business cards
- use "early bird" registration to save money
- plan the kinds of connections you want to make
- learn more about the presenters and identifiy those who are the most dynamic speakers
- create a daily schedule for yourself
- check out any special interest groups within the conference
- check the weather forecast; pack shoes and clothing that are professional-looking and comfortable for all day wear
- volunteer to introduce a speaker or serve as a panel moderator or discussant
- to get started presenting, try a poster session
- check into sources of travel support at your institution
- set a purpose; for example, getting materials to support you in a new teaching assignment
- generate a list of questions that you want answered during the meeting

During the Conference

- arrive early if possible and pick up your materials ahead of the crowd
- determine if the conference has an app and use it to stay updated
- at the start of each day, check any last-minute changes to sessions
- read name tags and engage others in informal conversation (e.g., on the elevator, waiting in line)
- introduce yourself to others without being too bold or interrupting other conversations
- follow the conference on social media (e.g., hashtag)
- excuse yourself gracefully if a conversation is unpro-ductive
- schedule times for extended conversations with important contacts, during meals or breaks
- visit the booths of publishers to review their materials and identify outlets for written work
- when others share a business card or e-mail, accept it graciously and store them in the same place
- rather than racing around to as many sessions as possible, be selective

After the Conference

- review all of the materials gathered at the conference and decide what ito keep and what to discard
- organize valuable materials from the conference into a binder or electronic files
- within a few days after the meeting, e-mail important new acquaintances
- if you are traveling by air or rail, use this time to think about improvements to your presentation
- share what you have learned with interested colleagues and students
- if the conference was productive, check the deadline and consider submitting a proposal to conduct a session for next year
- reflect on some ways that you can become more involved, such as committee service or running for office
- if you have made a plan to collaborate with someone else, follow through before too much time elapses

Fig. 1.2 Ways to make the most of participation in conferences

In addition to attending presentations of others' research, he or she might also do such things as, attend a panel discussion conducted by journal editors on writing for publication and visit the bulletin boards and conference display tables to collect calls for papers that might be suitable outlets for his or her research. Figure 1.2 suggests ways to make the most of conference participation.

The experiences amassed attending conferences as a participant are a good starting point for developing skill as a presenter (Freudenberg et al. 2008). They keep us in touch with "the other side of the podium," the audience, and this is a very necessary part of making effective presentations.

Activity: Best/Worst Presentation Experiences

Everyone has no doubt had both good and bad experiences with presentations. Analyzing them can point out what needs to be done as well as things to be avoided. Make a list of the characteristics of the best/worst sessions you have attended.

When describing the worst presentations, people frequently mention failings that would be attributable to lack of preparation (e.g., being misinformed/uninformed), ineffective use of the time allotted (e.g., spending 30 min on an introductory activity and rushing through the remaining, more important tasks), inadequate evidence (e.g., recommending practices without providing research support), and poor audience awareness (e.g., presenting something that obviously was developed for another purpose/audience, such as a dissertation defense). Also on the negative side are personal characteristics that include such things as distracting habits, insincerity, arrogance, impracticality of ideas, or being dismissive of participants' questions. For helpful advice on making professional presentations, see Michael E. Smith's Publishing Archaeology blog (http://publishingarchaeology.blogspot.com/).

In the best presentations, the presenter is knowledgeable, well planned, makes effective use of time, and offers research-based recommendations. Effective presenters are polished, poised professionals and achieve a "meeting of the minds" with the audience. The audience feels as though they know the presenter and that the presenter cares to know them. Reciprocal trust and respect is built, despite the fact that they are together for a relatively short period of time. Effective presenters also are a "good fit" with the conference in terms of demeanor and appearance; if the conference is very formal, they match that level and if the event is more casual, they accommodate to that tone.

Elements of Effective Speaking—From the Ancient Greeks

One source for understanding what makes an oral presentation effective harkens all the way back to Ancient Greece. Throughout history, the most celebrated skills in oratory have been attributed to Greek orators such as Aristotle and Socrates. When preparing to become public speakers who were capable of persuading others, the Greeks relied on three elements of effective speaking; ethos (sincerity, integrity credibility), pathos (the human element, emotional appeal of the message, and relevance to the real world) and logos (the persuasiveness of the argument and the quality of the evidence) (www.ethospathoslogos.com). The meaning of these terms is reflected in three words in common use today: ethical, empathic, and logical.

More often than not, when one professional is presenting to another, the goal is to convince participants to change their behaviors in ways that will make their daily practice more effective. Presenters often endorse a new teaching strategy, suggest better ways of dealing with difficult clients, or demonstrate how to use a technology tool. Yet changing a habit involves ego threats, such as the risk of exposing ignorance or of failing at a task. Most people need to be encouraged in the original sense of that French word—to "give heart"—before they will attempt to modify behavior. Most of us will not attempt something new unless the odds are stacked in our favor, unless we think—as social psychologist Gilbert Brim (2000) suggests–that we have at least an 80 % chance of success. Highly effective presenters urge us to try. They lead by example. They are honest about the challenges. They neither exaggerate the difficulties in the interest of making themselves "look good" nor do they gloss over potential problems. They also have sufficient expertise to spare us at least some of the beginner's mistakes. In fact, Werner Heisenberg, a Nobel Prize Laureate in physics, once said that "An expert is someone who knows the worst mistakes that can be made in a field and, how to avoid them."

When we invite doctoral students to plan their first conference workshop, many allocate 10–15 min of a one-hour session to brainstorming. Perhaps this is because that is what they have experienced themselves, an expedient way of producing a plan, or a lack of confidence in their expertise. Whatever the reason, the common practice of assembling a group of professionals at a conference and devoting a large portion of time to brainstorming is not recommended. Most conference participants expect a session that uses the presenter's expertise to "fast forward" to research-based strategies and possible solutions. They will be dissatisfied with listing random ideas because it does not advance their thinking at a satisfying pace

Audience Awareness: The Key to Successful Presentations

Conference attendees are a diverse group of learners. A mismatch occurs when presenters disregard this and decide to rely exclusively on the approach that they prefer. This happens, for example, when researchers become so immersed in their data and are so enthused about the topic that that they fail to consider other points of view—such as the implications for practice. Just as proposal writers are advised to be client-centered in order to secure grant funding, presenters need to be participant-centered in order to get positive session evaluations.

In *The Presenter's Fieldbook: A Practical Guide,* Robert Garmston (2005) argues that a single audience actually consists of four different audiences. He refers to them as (1) scientists, (2) inventors, (3) professors and (4) friends. Figure 1.3 explains these four audiences and their dominant goal for attending a professional presentation.

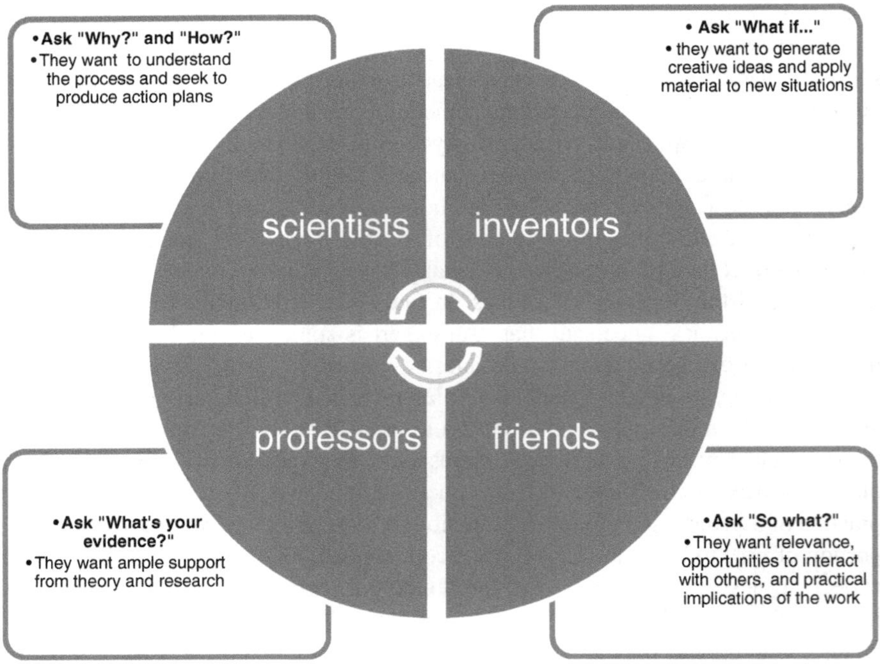

Fig. 1.3 *The four audiences* (adapted from Garmston 2005)

Activity: Planning for Different Audiences in a Professional Workshop or Training

1. What is the theme of the conference? What is the topic of your conference session?
2. Begin by writing 3–5 *participant-centered* outcomes; remember, these are not stated as what you will do. In other words, how will the participants benefit (beyond the getting information) and what will they do (beyond sit and listen)?
3. Consider Garmston's (2005) four audiences—those who want to formulate ideas (scientists), those who demand evidence (professors), those who want to affiliate with other professionals (friends), and those who want to get creative (inventors). What have you planned that would engage each of these groups?

Online Resources on Benefits of Conference Participation

The Savvy Grad Student Guide to Conference Networking
abdsurvivalguide.com/archives/2013-01-22.htm

In this All-But-Dissertation Survival Guide article offers advice to doctoral students on the value of participating in professional conferences.

How to Network at a Conference: 9 Steps (with Pictures)
http://www.wikihow.com/Network-at-a-Conference
This practical guide is written from a business perspective and organized into three phases: getting ready to network, making an impression, and following up.

Tips for Making Attending a Professional Conference More Valuable
http://ryanorilio.wordpress.com/2013/02/01/how-to-make-attending-a-professional-conference-a-more-valuable-experience/
Teacher/photographer Ryan Orilio offers practical advice on using advanced technology to maximize the conference experience.

Mastering Your Ph.D.: Making the Most of a Conference
http://sciencecareers.sciencemag.org/career_magazine/previous_issues/articles/2007_03_23/caredit.a0700039
Book authors Noordam and Gosling offer sound advice to doctoral candidates entering into the conference venue.

Conferences: Why to Attend and How to Benefit
www.iarr.org/storage/newprofessionals/conferences.pdf
Practical advice on capitalizing on the networking aspects of conferencing.

Attending an Academic Conference
homes.cs.washington.edu/ ~ mernst/advice/conference-attendance.html
Advice for first-time conference attendees about building a professional network.

Professionalism Among Presenters

Behaving professionally has two major aspects: ways of communicating and physical appearance. In terms of communication, the emphasis is on courtesy and respect. For more details on professional communication, review *Handbook for Effective, Professional Communication* at http://www.esf.edu/fnrm/documents/FNRM_Communications_Handbook2008.pdf.

If you are traveling to another country, be certain to do your homework and learn about their customs, particularly with regard to ways of greeting one another, proximity to others, and what types of touch are permitted. Some conference participants are under the mistaken impression that behaving professionally applies only to other professionals or to those they hope to impress. To illustrate, a keynote speaker who was a leader in the field of multicultural education and inclusion was in the ladies' room in an Atlanta hotel. The room was staffed by an African American housekeeper who kept the area neat and handed people paper towels to dry their hands; there was a basket for tips on the counter. When the housekeeper handed this noted speaker a towel, she completely ignored her and did not bother to leave a tip. Then the housekeeper noticed that the famous speaker had left her hat on the counter and rushed out into the hallway to return it to her. Again, this supposed leader in multicultural education kept talking to her companions and took the item without even pausing to say thank you. Clearly, the leading researcher's actions were very inconsistent with her message. When attending a professional conference, extend courtesy and respect to everyone. This includes the hotel staff, taxi drivers, support personnel, or the homeless person sitting on the sidewalk. You are functioning as a representative of your profession and your actions will affect that group's reputation in the larger community. There can be many frustrating experiences with travel, such as a hotel that overbooks the rooms, mistakes on scheduling the shuttle to the airport, or overcrowded restaurants. Strive for grace under pressure rather than having a meltdown, as this probably will do nothing to improve the predicament. While it is fine to describe what would resolve the issue, it is not acceptable to be disrespectful and discourteous.

Proper presentation attire is another aspect of professionalism. Those who are making the presentation should be a little bit dressed up, not necessarily in the sense of the height of fashion, but in the sense of looking polished and professional. There is almost no professional conference session where tattered jeans, flip flops, exercise attire, or provocative clothing are worn. At some conferences, there even may be events that require formal wear, for example, an awards dinner. One simple way to determine what is expected is to look at the photos from the previous year's conference. Sometimes, graduate students have been living in blue jeans and do not own professional clothes. If this is the case and finances are a concern, try a discount or overstock store or a clothing resale shop. Even on the airplane, wear something basic that you could wear as a conference participant in case your suitcase gets lost. You do not need a fabulous wardrobe; one suit and different shirts/ties or blouses/scarves probably is sufficient for a short conference. If you have little experience with professional dress, ask someone to advise you.

Ethical Issues in Conference Presentations

Presenters at conferences need to make ethical decisions that show respect for the time, money, and effort of fellow professionals. To illustrate, an assistant professor with very little travel support from her university decided to attend a preconference institute on qualitative research methods. This necessitated paying for another day at the hotel and an additional registration fee. She arrived at the session early, only to overhear the two presenters hastily attempting to organize the day. Statements such as "Oh, I thought *you* were doing that part" and "No, I didn't make copies of it" continued as the room began to fill. A full 10 min after the designated start time of 8:00 a.m., one presenter announced, "Becoming an observer is the most important part of conducting qualitative research. So, we want everyone to take advantage of being in downtown Atlanta. Take your pencil and a notebook and just write down what you see. We'll convene back in this room at 10:00." As you might predict, quite a few members of the group did not return. Several went to the conference headquarters table to lodge a complaint or submitted a very negative evaluation of the session. Situations such as this one are inexcusable; no presenter should arrive at the site unprepared.

Another type of problem with conference presentations is that the presenter anticipated completing a project or study but did not complete the requisite work. Under these conditions, the ethical decision is to cancel, well in advance of the publication of the conference program. It is not ethical to attend and fail to fulfil the promise of the session description in the self-interest of "adding a line" to the curriculum vitae. Likewise, it is irresponsible for a "big name" professor to submit sessions to various conferences or multiple sessions at the same conference without any intention of attending and send graduate students make the presentation. If a name is on the session, that person should be in attendance unless there is some sort of emergency. The conference planners have every right to expect that all persons listed as presenters are, indeed, acting in good faith and will be there.

Yet another professional dilemma with respect to conference sessions is "re-cycling"–making the same presentation again and again. Doing this disappoints conference attendees who may be very interested in a particular topic and attend both sessions, only to discover that it is a repeat of what was presented previously. Be aware too that savvy tenure and evaluation committees at universities often will require the applicant to document that a subsequent presentation is distinctive from a previous one. If two or more presentations are considered to be a duplication, they may be counted only as one.

Serving on a Conference Planning Committee

Another way to get involved with conferences is to serve on the conference planning committee. Most of the time, conference planners are volunteers rather than professional event planners. Many professional organizations have a conference planning committee and need additional help. This also qualifies as a professional service activity for college/university faculty members seeking tenure and promotion. The roles that you might fulfil are varied, so choose one that holds the greatest potential for fostering professional growth. If, for example, you have presented numerous workshop/training type sessions and now seek to present research, you might volunteer to review research proposals. If your goal is to network, you could pick up a keynote speaker at the airport, introduce presenters, serve as a session moderator, lead the discussion after a group of papers has been presented, or distribute and collect the session evaluation forms. Some online resources to guide conference planning include:

Online Resources About Conference Planning

Planning a Conference
www.extension.purdue.edu/extmedia/ACS_109.pdf
This simple guide from Purdue University explains the basics of conference planning.

How to Run Your Greatest Conference Ever
www.eitforum.com/6596.php
Advice from a professional conference planner on keys to success.

Planning and Organizing an Annual Conference
http://kmh-lanl.hansonhub.com/pc-26-123-potvin.pdf
This outline guides conference planners through the many tasks associated with planning a conference for a professional organization.

8 Ways to Make Your Conference More Successful
http://adulted.about.com/od/professionalcertifications/tp/8-Ways-To-Make-Your-Conference-More-Successful.htm
This About Education article highlights strategies for facilitating more networking at professional conferences.

Conclusion

The overarching purpose of conferences is to participate more fully in the ongoing professional dialogue. Both for the participants and the presenters, conferences represent a professional development opportunity. These opportunities occur not only during the formal sessions that appear in the conference program but also through informal networking that occurs when groups of professionals convene. As teacher/scholars make the transition from participating in conferences as audience members to participating as presenters of various types of sessions, it is important to keep the audience uppermost in mind. From an ethical standpoint, teacher/scholars need to approach conferences, not as a venue for shameless self-promotion, but with the hope of contributing the type of good, honest work that makes an enduring contribution to the field.

References

Brim, G. (2000). *Ambition: How we manage success and failure throughout our lives* (orig. pub. 1992). iUniverse.

Bruner, J. (1996). *The culture of education*. Cambridge, MA: Harvard University Press.

Ernst, M. (2004). *Attending an academic conference*. Retrieved May 1, from http://homes.cs.washington.edu/~mernst/advice/conference-attendance.html.

Fischer, B. A. (2006). *Attending professional meetings*. Retrieved May 1, 2015 from www.psm.edu/rise/.../Documents/Attendingprofessionalmeetings.pdf.

Freudenberg, B., Brimble, M., Vyvan, V. & Corby, D. (2008). A penny for your thoughts: Can participation in a student-industry conference improve students' presentation skills? *International Journal of Learning, 15*(5), 187–200. Retrieved June 9, 2015 from http://www98.griffith.edu.au/dspace/bitstream/handle/10072/20287/52025__1.pdf?sequence=1.

Garmston, R. (1997, 2005). *The presenter's fieldbook: A practical guide* (2nd ed.). Norwood, MA: Christopher-Gordon Publishers.

Hay, I., Dunn, K., & Street, A. (2005). Making the most of your conference journey. *Journal of Geography in Higher Education, 29*(1), 159–171.

Rébék-Nagy, G. (2008). The importance of conference presentations in higher education. *Problems of Education in the 21st Century, 7,* 99–106.

Tappe, M. K., & Galer-Unti, R. A. (2009). Health educators' role in promoting health literacy and advocacy for the 21st century. *Journal of School Health, 71*(10), 477–478. doi:10.1111/j.1746-1561.2001.tb07284.

Vega, R. D., & Connell, R. S. (2007). Librarians' attitudes toward conferences: A study. *College & Research Libraries, 68*(6), 503–515.

Chapter 2
Before the Conference: General Planning Strategies

At an international conference in East Africa, a doctoral student invited one of her professors to attend her session and critique her performance. After the doctoral student was introduced, she announced that it was her first presentation ever and that she was terribly nervous. She then proceeded to talk rapidly and pace back and forth, stopping periodically to grab a bottle of water and take huge gulps from it. Several problems were evident here. First, talking very rapidly is ill-advised, particularly for an international audience who may be listening in a language other than their first. Secondly, by referring to her inexperience, she undermined her own expertise with the participants when she was very knowledgeable about the topic. Third, by calling attention to her nervousness, she put the entire audience on watch for outward signs of anxiety and raised their level of discomfort. Fourth, the pacing and water drinking were a distraction.

This chapter guides readers through the planning processes that are essential to prevent such beginners' mistakes and conduct an effective conference session. With regard to session planning, the emphasis is on being participant-oriented and being clear about appropriate outcomes for those attending the session. Templates for a presenter's introduction, a brief session description, and a minute-by-minute session schedule are supplied. Criteria for self- and peer-evaluation of conference presentations are included. Finally, volunteer service as a reviewer of conference proposals is recommended as a way to more fully internalize expectations for presentation proposals. The first step is understanding your role.

Understanding the Presenter's Role

Rather than thinking of a conference presentation it as an event and a date on the calendar, treat it as a project. There are decades of research to suggest that adult learners approach important tasks as self-directed, informal projects (Merriam and Bierema 2013). When adults pursue learning projects, they tend to seek out all available resources in an effort to master the task, such as working with mentors and consulting resources. If, for instance, a person wants to acquire proficiency with language, it would be common to enrol in a class, talk with native speakers, read in

M.R. Jalongo and C. Machado, *Making Effective Presentations at Professional Conferences*, SpringerBriefs in Education,
DOI 10.1007/978-3-319-23174-7_2

the target language, watch captioned text videos, and listen to language instruction tapes with headphones. The same kinds of strategies can and should be applied in order to master the skills of presenting at conferences.

Put Your Audience First

At an education conference, one of the events was the national field directors forum at the Association of Teacher Educators (ATE)—a group that focuses on teacher preparation programs. This forum group consists of people who are responsible for arranging, managing, and evaluating student teaching placements throughout the United States. The first presenter was affiliated with a university in an urban setting and she had decided to do the "all about me" presentation. Because she focused entirely on her specific context and program, participants started to question how her recommendations applied to their situations. For example, her university was in an urban setting and student teachers were within walking distance of several public schools. How did this apply to the person in a rural area? Within a few minutes, the participants' attention appeared to wane; their questions had to do with what Hoff (1992) refers to as the WIIFM variable— "what's in it for me?" This is a common error of presenters. They find their own program so fascinating that they neglect to step back from it and talk about the more general lessons learned so that a diverse audience can glean something from it. Generally speaking, it is inappropriate to give exactly the same presentation to a national or international audience that you would give to local colleagues. Treat those who attend your session as you would honored guests at your home: attend to their needs, respect their wishes, help them to feel welcomed, and accommodate to their tastes and interests.

Introducing Yourself

Before planning any presentation, accept that your audience will be wondering:

- Who are you and how did you become knowledgeable about this?
- What is your topic and purpose?
- What facts, ideas, and skills will I acquire from participating?
- How does this topic relate to me?
- How can I apply this new information to my situation?
- What is in this for me? (Hoff 1992)

Activity: Write a Three-Sentence Introduction for Yourself

At many conferences, members of the organization volunteer to introduce speakers. The person introducing you will appreciate it if you have a *brief, easy to read* introduction prepared in advance. Some suggestions are:

1. Type it in 18-point print, double-spaced for ease of reading.
2. Keep the length to not more than 3 or 4 short sentences (approximately ½ page). (Note: for keynote speakers, more detail can be added—about one page is sufficient).
3. Provide some cues on the correct pronunciation of the first and last name (e.g., phonetic pronunciation, a common word that is pronounced that way, or "rhymes with").
4. Describe your work experience in a *very concise* fashion.
5. Vary the sentence structure (e.g., do not begin every sentence with the presenter's name or a pronoun).
6. Mention the presenter's current position (e.g., doctoral candidate, faculty member)
7. Conclude with the area of interest that led to making this presentation.

Differentiate Between Speeches and Presentations

Many people who are new to making conference presentations base their expectations on the speeches that they have heard at various community events. Even after they begin attending conferences, they may erroneously assume that their slot on the conference program is supposed to be more like the keynote address than the smaller group sessions. As a first step, presenters need to differentiate between speeches and presentations. This is outlined in Fig. 2.1.

Locating Suitable Venues

When seeking an outlet for a session presentation, there are several strategies for identifying possible groups and meetings.

- Think about cost associated with presenting at a conference. Be certain that you understand eligibility requirements and rules governing travel reimbursement. Many conferences have reduced registration fees for students or have a block of hotel rooms at reduced rates for those who register early. If funding is a concern, plan ways to reduce costs, such as carpooling to the site if feasible, sharing a room, or bringing some easily transportable, pre-packaged food rather than buying every meal at a restaurant.

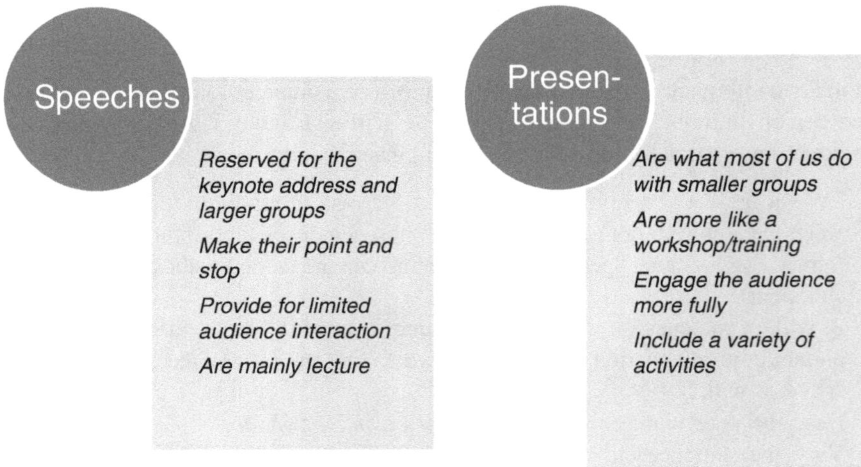

Fig. 2.1 The Difference between speeches and presentations

- Read the call for proposals very carefully to determine if your topic and approach is a match. For example, if a meeting for a group of counselors has the theme of family-centered practices, any session proposed needs to mesh with this goal.
- Begin with the professional organizations in which you hold membership. If you are relatively new to the field, talk with accomplished faculty members about the organizations in which they are active members or officers. Visit their websites to view a calendar of their national, regional, state, and local meetings. The publications of these organizations often publish calls for conference proposals and papers, so that is another place to look.
- From a professional development perspective, it is good to "stretch" and try to advance to the next level. So, after being accepted for a local conference is no longer a challenge, consider submitting a proposal at the state or regional level and, after presentations at the state and regional level are easy to accomplish, try for a national or international venue.
- Graduate students should check the postings in their academic departments because calls for conference proposals frequently are shared in this informal way. While you are attending a conference plan for the subsequent year. Usually, there are bulletin boards or tables with information that advertise other professional meetings, so be certain to peruse those materials.
- Faculty members seldom are fully funded for travel to professional conferences by their employers and usually, only featured speakers—such as invited keynote speakers—have their expenses paid by the sponsoring organization. Given this situation, presenters are free to choose whatever conference themes, formats, and locales, they find appealing. *The Chronicle of Higher Education* publishes a

conference calendar of different professional meetings in various disciplines in the October issue that can be a valuable resource for planning conference travel.

Selecting the Topic

How should you go about selecting a topic? Use the "Four Cs" in Table 2.1 to guide you through topic selection.

Choosing a Title

A good way to begin with writing the title for your session is by referring to a copy of a conference program from the previous year in hard copy or online. This will provide some sense of an appropriate title. In general, some guidelines are:

- Consider the audience and meeting theme
- Emphasize outcomes
- Identify concerns, issues, trends
- Match carefully to the session content
- Avoid cryptic titles that leave the audience wondering what to expect
- Stimulate interest and motivate attendance
- Do not invent forced acronyms

Table 2.1 The "Four Cs" of topic selection

1.	*Curiosity.* Effective presenters select a topic that they want to know more about. Everyone has attended a session that seems emotionally flat because the presenter's interest for the topic has waned or never existed. Audiences respond well when the presenter conveys enthusiasm for the topic
2.	*Competence.* Beginning presenters frequently are daunted by the fact that they are not the leading national expert on the subject. First and foremost, you can—in the words of Sir Issac Newton—"stand on the shoulders of giants". Figure out who the leading experts are and rely on their work for support. Remember that practical work experience is another type of expertise. When there are doubts about expertise, another helpful approach is to collaborate. Some of the best conference sessions are presented by teams of professionals who represent different types of expertise, such as theory, research, and practice
3.	*Commitment.* Whatever topic you select, your interest in it will need to be sufficient to sustain you when investing additional time and effort into learning more about it. Avoid selecting a topic purely because it is a "hot topic" in the field. Make it clear why you selected the topic and why it should matter to others
4.	*Credibility.* Participants in a session should have the sense that they are in capable hands of someone who has plowed deeply into the literature and has direct experience related to the topic. Strive to show that you have something to offer beyond what is already widely available in the literature

Activity: Titles that Mesh with Conference Themes

One major clue to what organizations are seeking is to review their mission statements—often posted on websites as "About Us" or "History". Doing this provides insight into the group's goals. For example, The Society for Research in Child Development describes itself as follows:

> The Society is a multidisciplinary, not-for-profit, professional association with a membership of approximately 5,500 researchers, practitioners, and human development professionals from over 50 countries. The purposes of the Society are to promote multidisciplinary research in the field of human development, to foster the exchange of information among scientists and other professionals of various disciplines, and to encourage applications of research findings. Our goals are pursued through a variety of programs with the cooperation and service of our governing council, standing committees, and members. www.srcd.org/

Having this background helps prospective presenters to judge whether or not their proposal for a conference session will be a good fit. The second step is to read about the particular conference. Usually, there is a theme set by the conference planners and, if the proposed session meshes with that theme, this increases chances of acceptance. Locate both pieces of information—organizational mission and conference theme—for a conference at which you hope to present.

Identifying Outcomes for Participants

Just as teachers write objectives for learners, presenters need to generate outcomes for the participants. How will the attendees benefit beyond merely getting information? When you think about it, if information is the only outcome, this can be accomplished in a much more cost-effective fashion by staying home and reading. Therefore, try to focus on what is it that those who attend your session will accomplish beyond sitting and listening while you dispense information. This is a particularly important expectation for workshop/training types of sessions. Emphasize the higher-order thinking skills of application, analysis, synthesis, evaluation, and creativity. Even if you are presenting a research paper, shift the emphasis from merely reporting on a study to giving participants an insider's view of your work: why you pursued it, how it addresses a gap in the extant literature, how your design aligns with the research questions, and ways in which the study findings advance thinking in the field. As you plan, keep in mind the reasons that people take the time and invest the money in traveling to a conference. For example, they want to keep current in their fields, expand their professional repertoires, perform better in their teacher/scholar/researcher roles, have something interesting to talk about, form alliances with like-minded professionals, and advance their careers. The fundamental question to be answered has to do with "value added": How will participants benefit from spending time with you in your session?

Activity: Writing a Short Description for a Session

The great majority of conferences will require you write a brief description of your session suitable for publication in the conference program. Typically, there is a 50 word limit, so the description must be concise. Sessions that are not presentations of original research can be described using the following "formula":

1. Opening statement
   - Write a somewhat general (and fairly indisputable) statement about the situation.
2. Your approach, "take" on the issue, stance
   - Give participants a sense of the focus for the session.
3. Benefits *for the Participants*
   - What will they accomplish that they could not achieve by just reading? What will they do besides sit and listen? Begin each item in the list with a verb; list 3 or 4 main outcomes.
   - Write a final sentence about the resources that they will receive, such as an annotated list of websites, a checklist, or a synthesis of the research.

Organizing the Session

Psychologists refer to a phenomenon called the primacy and recency effect where human memory is concerned. As applied to a conference session, this means that participants are more likely to remember what happened first and last than what was in the middle. Effective presenters know this and pay particular attention to effective introductions and conclusions. So, when the only introduction is "Today I'm going to talk about…" and the conclusion is something such as "Okay, we are running out of time, so…", two very important opportunities to get the message across have been squandered.

Engaging Introductions

Begin with a thought-provoking experience that focuses attention. Some strategies for a strong introduction are:

- A set of questions
- A real life account or a case

- A show of hands survey
- Startling statistics or surprising facts
- A paradox
- A list of concerns generated by the group
- A concrete object or prop
- A simulation or "test."

Effective Conclusions

Some ways to arrive at effective conclusions are:

- *Alert participants to the conclusion.* When participants hear words such as "Finally…", "In conclusion…" or "To summarize…" this tends to refocus attention.
- *Restate the main thesis.* Remind participants of the "take away" message that was their primary purpose for the session. For example, at the end of a presentation on writing for professional publication for novices conducted by five author/editors, the panel moderator said, "Our goal here today was to demystify the process of writing for publication so that 'new voices' can join the ongoing professional dialogue. We look forward to receiving the new and improved manuscripts you have developed after following the recommendations we've shared. If your schedule permits, we also hope to see you at our editor roundtables tomorrow to discuss specific ideas for journal articles."
- *Reflection.* Everything that you have shared will not be equally useful to all, so plan a concluding activity that encourages participants to think about what they have learned and plan to implement it. During a workshop you might ask participants to list three strategies that they will implement immediately and three that they plan to try later on. For a longer session, you might invite participants to write the questions that they still have at the midpoint on note cards, quickly review/categorize them, and respond to each one.
- *Evaluation.* Many times, a session will conclude with a request for participants to complete a short evaluation form that is collected by a member of the conference committee. Be certain to allocate sufficient time for attendees to do this before the next presenter and group is waiting out in the hallway. Ask if you are permitted to review the evaluations before they are whisked away because few conferences take the time to compile and share the results. If no evaluation is planned, do your own so that you can improve (Rogoschewski 2011).

Activity: Basic Evaluation of a Conference Session

Try presenting your session to a group prior to the conference, such as a college class. Ask them to evaluate the presentation using the Likert scale below or adapt the scale to suit your situation.

1. The presenter was well prepared				
Strongly agree	Agree	Undecided	Disagree	Strongly disagree
2. The session was well organized				
Strongly agree	Agree	Undecided	Disagree	Strongly disagree
3. The presentation held my interest				
Strongly agree	Agree	Undecided	Disagree	Strongly disagree
4. I learned something of value from the session				
Strongly agree	Agree	Undecided	Disagree	Strongly disagree
5. I would attend other sessions conducted by this presenter or recommend this one to a colleague interested in this topic				
Strongly agree	Agree	Undecided	Disagree	Strongly disagree
Comments:				

Writing the Proposal

Many people learn how to write conference proposals primarily through trial and error. Others have the advantage of support from an experienced, successful presenter to orient them to the process, collaborate with them, and/or supply them with examples to follow. Still others approach making presentations as they would conducting a review of the literature; they search for published resources that will provide them with guidance.

A faculty member arrived at a doctoral seminar and shared a call for proposals to present at the state-level conference of a leading professional organization in their field. After several students inquired about how to write the proposal, their advisor posted two examples of her own successful proposals and, with the permission of former students from the class, two additional session proposals. Because the main purpose of the conference was professional development for practitioners in the field, the typical session format was a one-hour workshop/training on a timely topic. The current students pored over these examples as if they were maps that showed the way to buried treasure. What did they notice? First, the language was surprisingly direct; the proposal was not written in the same style as their class papers or dissertations. It was evident that clear communication of ideas was the goal. Second, that the writing was more like writing a grant in that it was focused on benefits for the participants. As a result, the conference guidelines required that prospective presenters include 3–5 outcomes for participants. Third, the activities were varied and engaging; all four of the sample proposals that students reviewed were interesting and persuaded the reader that the session merited a place on the program. In many ways, the proposal was more like a lesson plan in that it reflected elements of good teaching, such as including individual, small group, and total group activities. Finally, the sample proposals followed the required format exactly and were so carefully crafted and proofread that they were error free.

Mapping Out the Session

Consider the following points as you plan:

- How much time do I have?
- How formal/informal is the event?
- What is the room set up?
- What has been particularly successful with this audience in the past?
- What kinds of visual aids are acceptable?
- What types of technology are available?
- Who is paying for and responsible for what?
- What criteria will be used to evaluate my performance?

Mapping out a session will require you to:

- State the purpose for the session in audience-centered terms.
- Prepare a minute-by-minute schedule of activities
- Form a plan to immediately grab the audience's interest
- Identify a list of benefits for participants that go beyond the knowledge level to analysis, application, synthesis, evaluation and creative responses.
- Design an activity to attain each outcome.
- Consider the four audiences: those who want facts, to be creative, to interact with others, and to work with ideas (Garmston 2005).
- Develop a strategy to ascertain if the intended outcomes were achieved
- Plan an effective conclusion that underscores the purpose for the session (Table 2.2)

Activity: Review of a Minute-by-Minute Plan for a Conference Session

Use this set of criteria to self-evaluate your minute-by-minute session plan or ask a peer to evaluate your proposal with this set of questions.

Table 2.2 Example of minute-by-minute session plan

Creating and sharing video lessons:
improving student math achievement with a "flipped classroom" approach
Theresa McQuaide
Session description:
Creating and sharing video lessons that learners can use to practice outside of classroom time is one way to support student achievement in mathematics. Participants in this session will observe examples of the "flipped classroom" approach while being introduced to some Web 2.0 tools that will allow them to create and share their own resources for the classroom. Each participant will use the free software presented to create a short video.

Time allocated (min)	**Goals for participants**	**Presenter's activity**
5	Technology check at work station	Introduce and distribute handouts. Seat participants at computer work stations; verify that the shortcuts are accessible
3	Understand the flipped classroom and its potential as a teaching tool	Use research to identify the features and uses of a flipped classroom
3	Observe a flipped classroom in action	Demonstrate Henrico County public school math site. http://teachers.henrico.k12.va.us/math/HCPSAlgebra1/module4-4.html
10	Review a major repository of resources for teaching mathematics	Demonstrate www.Kahnacademy.org. Show the concept map, practice and video library. Participants will try a practice exercise, using the hint and video lesson features to identify homework suitable for their students
5	Learn how to create and share video files	A handout on how to use the free site Edmodo.com will guide in uploading their videos or links. Participants will create a login at tappedin.org and a link to Kahn Academy
5	Use software to create instructional videos	Show how to use Camstudio, Paint and Geogebra to record a video
20	Create a 1 minute video	Attendees will create a video, save the file on the desktop and save it at the Edmodo site.
4	Make a plan to implement what was learned and evaluate the workshop	Participants will complete an online survey at Zoomerang on how they will apply what they have learned during the session to their teaching of mathematics

Instructions for the Author of the Proposal:

Please write this information on your conference proposal copies if you have not done so already:

Who is the intended audience? What professional organization are you considering as the venue for sharing this material? What particular type of session do you have in mind (e.g., workshop, panel discussion, research report, and so forth)?

Reviewer's Criteria

- Does the title accurately reflect the content? Does it set participants' expectations appropriately? If you can think of a way to improve the title, suggest it.
- Is the brief description clear? Does it sound interesting and worthwhile? What suggestions do you have for improving the brief description? Please feel free to edit it right on the copy or offer specific suggestions.
- Is there a clear sense of how participants will benefit from investing their conference time in this session? Please make a list of at least 3 benefits you would expect as a participant in this session.
- VERY IMPORTANT: What will participants do besides sit and listen? Please offer some ideas for making the session interactive.
- What questions would you expect to have answered in a session with this title and description? Please list several.
- What understandings and skills might you hope to acquire? Please identify some realistic outcomes, given the time constraints.
- What types of discussion, experiences, activities, simulations, cases, or examples might you hope to engage in during the session? Please provide some examples.
- What resources would be helpful? What would you hope the presenter might distribute in a handout? Please list some suggestions.
- What would be your worst fear about a session on this topic? Explain what the presenter could do to avert this.

Choosing and Using Examples

A professor of education was invited to give a keynote address on teaching children to read. The concept behind the conference was that experts on early literacy would share their divergent perspectives on the most effective ways to maximize literacy growth. First on the agenda was a proponent of intensive phonics instruction. She set forth the argument that, if only teachers would emphasize the sound structure of language earlier and lead children in "cracking the code", many reading problems would be averted. The next person to speak was a proponent of more balanced approaches and contended that this was a more effective way to reach and teach diverse groups of children because not all of them would have strength in listening to and interpreting the sound structure of language. She shared an example taken directly from the written work of a child who had failed kindergarten and failed again in first grade due to poor reading scores. In the child's handwriting, there was this word: flicewatur. She asked the audience of teachers to analyze the word from a phonics perspective. This child who had been unsuccessful with reading used a blend, (fl) a silent e (ice), and a r—controlled vowel (ur) but she still did not spell the word she had in mind—flyswatter–in a conventional way. A picture from the child's journal truly was, as the old saying goes, worth 1000 words.

When choosing examples to illustrate key concepts, realize that the human brain responds most strongly to powerful visual images, seeks patterns in complexity, and "runs" on stories (Jensen 2006). Long after the session is over, these are the things that people will still remember, so harness the power of these tools as you plan. Sometimes speakers attempt to use some of the tired, old ways of connecting with an audience—telling a joke, describing what happened to them on the trip there, showing a bunch of cartoons, or a silly "icebreaker". These strategies can backfire. The joke can fall flat or offend someone. The trip there may have been uneventful, the cartoons copyrighted, and the icebreaker may set an inappropriate tone and expectations for the session. Any examples that you choose must, at the very least, be suitable for the occasion, of interest to the audience, and relevant to the topic of the presentation. Gimmicks are to be avoided. For instance, one presenter began a session with a series of true/false questions about herself, such as "Was Dr. X named Pennsylvania's Teacher of the Year?" This did not have the intended effect of establishing credibility, however. It came across as ego because it used several minutes of the session.

Teaching with Cases

The case method originated in the teaching of law and medicine, was extended to business, and is now used in a wide range of disciplines. Cases bring real world situations into the session, provide a shared experience to stimulate discussion, raise interesting questions without simple answers, encourage professionals to reflect on actions, and demand decisions that rely on professional wisdom (Davis 2009). In general, it is preferable to invent your own cases rather than "borrow" someone else's. There are at least three reasons for this. First of all, a published case may be familiar to some participants already. Secondly, you may not be qualified to answer questions that surface about someone else's case. Third, by writing your own cases from your experiences, you build credibility with an audience.

Activity: Creating Your Own Cases

- Review the published cases of others before attempting to write your own.
- Identify cases that engage participants intellectually and emotionally.

- Set outcomes for the participants and decide how and when the cases will be used.
- Protect the confidentiality of the people in the case.
- Keep the cases engaging but brief so that they can be read in few minutes' time.
- Try out, revise, and try again.

Each case will need:

1. Setting–describe the who, what, when, and where of the situation. Include only those things that are essential to understanding the point of the story.
2. Beginning–Start with something that will get the reader interested in reading the case. It is not necessary to arrange things chronologically; you can begin with the most interesting part.
3. Account–Do more than summarize the event. Carefully select some details that made the incident memorable, such as a verbatim comment, nonverbal behavior, etc.
4. Reflection—Encourage reflection on the professional's role in the situation using thought-provoking questions.
5. Outcome– Describe the consequences of the incident for the client or learner.
6. Ending–Every story needs to build to a satisfying conclusion. Note that the outcome need not be shared until after the discussion has occurred. The decisions reached and justification for those decisions are important.

Some questions that might be used when discussing cases are:

- What possibilities for action are there?
- What are the consequences of each for the various stakeholders?
- What should ___ do at the first decision point?
- How did ___ get into this predicament?
- If you were a friend of ____, what advice might you have given?
- What actions should be taken?
- What concepts, principles, or theories seem to follow from this analysis?

Activity: Evaluation of a Case Study

Use the following checklist to assess a case that you have written or one written by a peer.

YES	NO
Content: the case includes a setting, beginning, account, reflection, outcome, and conclusion	
YES	NO
Purpose: The case identifies how it is linked to session goals	
YES	NO

(continued)

(continued)

Impact: the case tells a real story that is emotionally compelling and memorable; it is rich in characterizations and promotes empathy with the central characters	
YES	NO
Relevance: The case focuses on professional dispositions and appropriate courses of action.	
YES	NO
Challenging: The case lacks an obvious or clear-cut right answer and raises interesting questions and dilemmas; it allows for competing interpretations of motives. It engages professionals intellectually and encourages them to provide a rationale for their point of view	
YES	NO
Clarity: The case is sufficiently clear and concise to prevent readers from becoming lost in extraneous details	
YES	NO
Organization: The case supplies details on how it will be introduced, explains how participants will work on the case, includes thought-provoking discussion questions, and plans how participants will report their responses	
YES	NO
Conclusion: The case provides participants with the actual outcome so that they can compare/contrast it with their own decisions	
YES	NO
Quality of Writing: The case is well written, carefully proofread, and free of mechanical errors	

At the Conference Site

After you have planned your presentation carefully and been accepted to the program, there are several things that you can do to have a successful conference experience.

1. *Check in at the conference desk.* Most conference planners have a separate registration area for presenters. Many require you to be an active member of the organization and wear a badge to enter the conference hall. Be aware that there may have been changes to the preliminary conference program. So, if at all possible, arrive early to get your badge, double-check the time and location of your presentation, and look at the room equipment/set up.
2. *Study the program.* Instead of spending all of your time with colleagues, branch out. Mark the conference program using a 1st/2nd choice strategy for various time slots in case there is a cancellation or the session is closed. Use breaks and meals to meet with key individuals and broaden your network. Large conferences typically have a name index in the back of the program and this can be very helpful in locating other presenters. If your goal is to speak with an acquisitions editor about a possible book, try visiting the booths at a time when they will be less busy, such as during a keynote address that you would not mind

missing. Remember that, if you plan to speak with an editor about a book project, you'll probably have not more than a minute or two to present your concept for the book. Instead of "showing what you know" and barraging the editor with jargon, emphasize how your book would represent a stride forward and be marketable. Think of it as a 1 or 2 min "commercial" for your book idea.

3. *Take time to review.* It is commonplace to have a sleepless night before the day of an important presentation. One worry you can address easily is fear of oversleeping. Take along a small travel alarm, set the alarm on a cellphone, and schedule a hotel wake-up call 10 min after that. Have all of your materials assembled. Place them against the inside of your hotel room door so that you cannot leave without picking them up. Even if you have practiced extensively, you'll want to go over your notes prior to the session, so if you wake up early and cannot go back to sleep, use this time to practice instead of tossing and turning. Use your visual aids, practice out loud (unless you are sharing a room!) and time yourself.
4. *Be considerate.* Arrive early enough to meet the person introducing you and share your brief introduction with that person. If you are on a panel and do not know the other presenters, be certain to introduce yourself to them. Even if someone else is the timekeeper, bring along your own way of monitoring the time. Keep in mind that attendees at your session need time to get to the next scheduled event. The presenters who have the room after you probably are waiting out in the hallway will appreciate it if you do not exceed your time slot. If there are conversations after the session, move away from the front of the room to allow the next presenters to get set up.
5. *Prepare to speak.* Make a deliberate effort to breathe deeply and relax (Hardicre et al. 2007). If you are very tense, your face may show it. One tip is to imagine that you are smelling something wonderful—roses, cookies. This helps to "soften" your facial expression so that you don't look as though you are scowling or disagreeing with the other speakers. Take discreet sips of water prior to beginning to speak because it is common for your throat to become dry when you are nervous. If you are on a panel, do not get so preoccupied with your own presentation that you neglect to listen to what others say. Think about what the others are saying, not only as a way of showing respect but also as a way to avoid the very embarrassing mistake of revealing that you were not listening by repeating something that was discussed already. Jot down notes if there is something that you'd like to comment on later, during the discussion period.
6. *Respond to questions with aplomb.* Many times, it is difficult for everyone to hear a question so one public speaking tip is to repeat or rephrase the question. After you are certain that you understand the question, respond directly to it. If there is no definitive answer to a question and oppositional points of view prevail, make this clear. If there is an answer but you don't know it, ask others to weigh in or offer to look into it further. Try to determine the underlying reason for a question. Sometimes, a person really does not have a question; rather, he or she wants to be acknowledged as a fellow expert. If a person asking a question

knows more about a particular aspect than you do, there is no disgrace in accepting this, thanking them, and moving on. You might try statements such as: "It sounds like you have extensive experience with…" "Thank you for pointing out…", or, if it is a digression and is taking too long (and you honestly feel this way), "I'd like to talk with you more afterwards if you have the time."

7. *Remember to say thank you.* Be gracious and convey appreciation to those who have participated and facilitated the presentation. Thank the audience, the person who introduced you, co-presenters, and hotel staff who helped you. If, for example, a staff member went above and beyond to help with a technology issue, take the time to fill out a comment card. If the presentation was during a meal and the food was exceptionally good and beautifully presented, let this be known to the management.
8. *Follow up.* As you get ready to leave the conference, review the contacts you made and keep your promises. If, for example, you ran out of handouts and gathered an e-mail list so that participants could get a copy, you need to do this even though your work duties have been piling up in your absence. If you exchanged business cards and agreed to make contact, do this within a few days' time. If you received constructive criticism on a work-in-progress, take the time to summarize it and make a plan for revising your paper. When papers are to be submitted for consideration as conference proceedings, study the guidelines. Submit the work in the required format and in a timely fashion.

Conclusion

Planning a presentation consists of six action steps: (1) selecting a topic, (2) analyzing and adapting to an audience, (3) conducting effective research and using online resources appropriately, (4) organizing the session with an outline, (4) using presentational aids effectively, (5) making choices about language, and (6) determining the delivery style (Verderber et al. 2014). Neglecting to consider any of these tasks is apt to lead to a less-than-successful outcome.

Online Resources: General Advice on Presenting

Sharp, E. (2014), Make your convention presentation shine. *COAHPERD Journal, 39*(2), 2.

How to Make a Good Presentation—Roger Darlington's World
http://www.rogerdarlington.me.uk/Presentation.html
Practical advice on preparing and presenting a conference session.

Giving a Conference Talk
http://courses.cs.washington.edu/courses/cse561/02au/notes/goodtalk.pdf
The basics for those who are new to making presentations.

Tips on Writing Successful Conference Presentation Proposals
http://blog.tesol.org/tips-on-writing-successful-conference-presentation-proposals/
McVeigh offers advice on the whole process of generating effective conference presentations.

What's the Difference between Making a Speech and Presenting a Paper?
https://nicholadgutgold.wordpress.com/2010/03/22/whats-the-difference-between-making-a-speech-and-presenting-a-paper/
A step-by-step guide to presenting a research paper.

Learn from the Experts
www.dailymotion.com
This compilation of videos offers advice to presenters; just type in "conference presentations" to identify a specific topic.

Florida Reading Association
http://www.flreads.org/Annual%20Conference/annual.htm
A good example of guidelines that conference planners develop to assist presenters in generating a successful proposal and conducting an effective session.

What to Expect Presenting at an Academic Conference
https://ferswriteshoe.wordpress.com/2012/02/13/what-to-expect-presenting-at-an-academic-conference/
A student presenting at a conference for the first time gives a detailed explanation of the process.

Presenting Your Work to Others: Social Work Career Center
http://careers.socialworkers.org/documents/Presenting%20Your%20Work%20to%20Others.pdf
Sage advice for presenters from the National Association of Social Workers.

Writing the Academic Conference Proposal
http://www.gradhacker.org/2011/06/01/writing-the-academic-conference-proposal/
Good advice from student Jennifer Sano-Franchini about writing conference proposals, complete with examples. There are many more resources at the GradHacker site.

References

Davis, B. (2009). *Tools for teaching* (2nd ed.). San Francisco, CA: Jossey-Bass.

Garmston, R. (2005, 1997). *The presenter's fieldbook: A practical guide* (2nd ed.). Norwood, MA: Christopher-Gordon Publishers.

Hardicre, J., Coad, J., & Devitt, P. (2007). Ten steps to successful conference presentations. *British Journal of Nursing, 16*(7), 402–404.

Hoff, R. (1992). *I can see you naked: The fearless guide to presenting*. Kansas City, MO: Andrews McMeel Publishing.

Jensen, E. (2006). *Enriching the brain: How to maximize every learner's potential*. San Francisco: Jossey-Bass.

Merriam, S. B., & Bierema, L. L. (2013). *Adult learning: Linking theory and practice*. San Francisco, CA: Jossey-Bass.

Rogoschewski, T. L. (2011). Developing a conference presentation: A primer for new library professionals. *Partnership*, *6*(2), 1–6. https://journal.lib.uoguelph.ca/index.php/perj/article/view/1573/2283#.VjYzPzZdGUk

Verderber, R., Sellnow, D., & Verderber, K. (2014). *The challenge of effective speaking in a digital age*. Boston, MA: Cengage Learning.

Chapter 3
Developing Confidence and Skill as a Presenter

Statistics from survey research indicates that fear of public speaking ranks alongside fear of dying for many people (see http://www.thefearofpublicspeaking.com). Even for experienced teachers and veterans of the conference circuit, making presentations can be daunting. This Chapter guides the reader in a self-evaluation of strengths as a presenter, ways to make the session more engaging for participants, and fielding difficult questions—all elements in developing skill as a presenter. In our experience as mentors, we find that graduate students and university faculty members sometimes have unrealistic expectations (e.g., a standing ovation for a speech or excellent ratings on every aspect of the session from all attendees). At the other end of the spectrum are individuals who have seen the apparent ease with which brilliant, vastly experienced presenters manage a session and mistakenly assume that minimal preparation is required. We counteract both misguided types of hopeful dreaming with the advice that presenters need to prepare thoroughly with the needs of the audience uppermost in their minds. This Chapter concludes with something that we have not seen discussed in any of the publications on presentation: how to rebound after a disappointing session.

Mastering General Presentation Skills

The international meeting of a large professional organization had, as one of its session formats, research symposia. Each session had a discussant/time keeper and four researchers, each with 15 min to present the highlights of their research. One session was particularly packed, with participants on the floor, leaning against the walls, and spilling out into the hallway on the 34th floor of the conference headquarters hotel. All of the presenters were relying on a laptop/projector set up to share their findings; however, with the third presentation, the projector malfunctioned, overheated, and started to smoulder. With quick thinking on the part of presenter four, electrical power to the projector was disconnected before it burst into flames and safety issues were addressed. Nevertheless, there was no equipment available for the fourth presenter's research findings.

M.R. Jalongo and C. Machado, *Making Effective Presentations at Professional Conferences*, SpringerBriefs in Education,
DOI 10.1007/978-3-319-23174-7_3

Although this is a dramatic example of things going wrong, the way to address such problems is by equipping yourself with multiple ways to share information. Always have an alternative to the preferred way and don't rely exclusively on one tool. For example, if a speaker is relying almost entirely on a video and, for whatever reason, it won't play, then what? In the case of the fourth research symposium presenter, she had made posters of the data and multiple copies of a three-page synopsis of the study. There weren't sufficient copies for the surprisingly popular session, so the data tables that had been enlarged at a print shop ended up being necessary too. As a direct result of having a backup plan, that 15 min presentation was very well-received.

The Importance of Planning

Thoughtful planning is the single, best way to avert presentation disasters. Perhaps the most fundamental type of planning is deciding what type of presentation suits you. Fortunately, for most professionals, there is a natural progression to acquiring skill as a presenter. Most teacher/scholars begin with small groups and are not involved in addressing large groups in an auditorium until they have amassed quite a bit of practice in other venues. In any case, speakers need to evaluate their strengths, limitations, and professional goals before they seek out or agree to different speaking engagements (Adler 2015). Giving an effective a presentation relies on a constellation of skills in research, organization, public speaking, interpersonal interaction, and intrapersonal awareness. Speakers need support to develop this complex repertoire of skills, so be certain to consult some highly-respected, comprehensive works on effective presentations (e.g., Sprague et al. 2015).

Some of the strategies that contribute to success with making presentations are:

1. *Gain information about the prior knowledge of the audience.* Participants are offended when speakers "talk down" to them and frustrated if the information is completely unfamiliar. The advantage of most conference sessions is that the audience chooses to be there rather than being required to attend. When in doubt, assume that they are at least interested in the topic and have acquired basic familiarity with the concept. If the group is small, you may want to take a moment to have each person state what they hope to accomplish by attending the session. Treat your session participants as you would respected colleagues.
2. *Emphasize what is original.* Many times, presenters devote far too much time to developing the background—particularly when sharing research. From a proportional allocation of time perspective, it is preferable to synthesize previous research and identify the gap that your study was designed to address. Discuss the contributions of the research rather than every possible data table. The challenge is to be thorough, yet concise.

3. *Personalize the information.* Highly effective presenters reveal something about themselves as professionals without being self-indulgent or confessional. The presentation should be more than a dull report. For example, when sharing research findings, a thought-provoking quotation from a person interviewed during the study or a surprising finding can be shared. Likewise, when conducting a workshop or training that is advocating a new and improved professional practice, describe a particular challenge and how it was addressed.
4. *Practice.* Presenters sometimes overlook the importance of rehearsing, timing, and critiquing a presentation. If you use presentation software, use at least 28 point print, keep information on each slide to no more than about 6 points, number the slides, provide a reference list, and proofread very carefully. Consider recording the presentation, asking a "critical friend" to review it, and critique it yourself (Happell 2009).

Improving Skills and Style

Effective presenters know that a successful session relies, not only on the message but also on the design and delivery of that message. "The Art and Science of a Successful Presentation" offers an annotated bibliography of resources centered on five features:

1. *Craft a strong message.* Identify the central message, split it up into mini-segments, edit ruthlessly, share details about the project context, make in memorable, and tell a story.
2. *Establish credibility.* Present a message backed by evidence, think through opposing viewpoints, and address them thoroughly and proactively.
3. *Plan informality.* Build rapport with the audience by briefly sharing something about yourself. Inject light-heartedness as appropriate into the presentation to open up the audience to receive new ideas.
4. *Design interactivity.* Generate thoughtful questions to engage the audience and maximize learning. Use questions as a way to connect with the audience, assess needs, get peer feedback, learn from others, and gather ideas for the future.
5. *Make delivery purposeful.* Use appropriate gestures, articulation, posture, voice, and talking speed. Use your audience's reactions to fine-tune your delivery as you go (American Evaluation Association 2015).

Print Resources on Improving Conference Presentations

Hafler, J. P. (2011). Effective presentations: Tips for success. *Nature Immunology, 12*(11), 1021–1023.

Hay, I., Dunn, K., and Street, A. (2005). Making the most of your conference journey. *Journal of Geography in Higher Education, 29*(1), 159–171.
Price, B. (2004). Effective learning number 22: Making a presentation. *Nursing Standard, 18*(39), 89–90.
Rzepczynski, M. (2014). Creating a great session presentation. *Public Libraries, 53* (2), 10–11.
Smith, D. T., and Salmond, R. (2011). Verbal sticks and rhetorical stones: Improving conference presentations in political science. *Political Science and Politics, 44*(3), 583–588.

Overcoming Fears

It is commonplace for speakers to feel anxious prior to an important presentation. Many times, the fears association with presenting a collection of "what ifs"—What if I trip and fall? What if I misspeak and make an embarrassing mistake? What if someone in the audience is harshly critical of my work? In all cases, the best defense against fears is to be proactive. Try to anticipate and prevent difficulties. For example, if you have rehearsed, checked and double-checked the equipment, and know the room, many worries about potential problems can be brought under control. When problems beyond your control surface, try not to make too much of them and take the approach that "the show must go on." If you state something incorrectly, pause briefly and correct it. In terms of worrying about audience members, it is helpful to remember that they want you to succeed—otherwise, their goals for attending your session will not be met. Do not take the advice of looking at a spot on the wall rather than at the session attendees' faces! It is better to look at a few friendly faces at first (e.g., people who are smiling or nodding encouragement) and scan the group periodically to determine how your message is being received. For example, a team of professors was presenting a session and, to their surprise, nearly 80 people attended the session. Originally, they expected a small group and had planned for each participant to introduce himself or herself; however, this would have taken far too much time. So, they informed the group of this decision and encouraged them to ask questions or offer comments at any time during the session. Afterwards, several participants thanked them for using their time together in the most productive way.

Coping with Nervousness

Accept that the sensation of "butterflies in the stomach" is commonplace and try not to dwell on it too much. Instead, think of channelling that nervous energy into an engaging presentation. In many cases, it is not so much feeling nervous as worry that the outward signs of nervousness will be on display. Some common manifestations and ways to address them follow.

1. *Difficulty getting started.* Many speakers report that those first few words are the hard part; after that, they are fine. Try something that will break the ice for you and your audience, without words. If it is a formal presentation, a slide with the title of your paper and your institutional affiliation can be posted. If is a less formal training or workshop, an image that is appropriate for the topic and audience can be used. You may also want to try something that gets the audience to respond in some way, for instance, if it is a large group, posing a question and having them answer by a show of hands or simply saying "good morning" enthusiastically and requesting a response.
2. *Fear of the unknown audience.* Speakers can be unnerved by the fear that someone is going to take issue with their material and begin an argument. One way to diminish such feelings is to arrive at the room well in advance of the session, get everything set up, and then greet people as they enter the room. Actually talking to a few people allows them to see you as a person and breaks down the sense that you are talking to a completely anonymous group. When you talk to a group, make eye contact and scan the room periodically. If it is a less formal gathering (e.g., a workshop rather than a keynote address), consider walking around the room as well, particularly when people are working in groups. This provides an opportunity to gauge how the activity is going and gives people a chance to ask a quick question or comment. When the group reconvenes as a whole, you can refer back to some of these conversations.
3. *A trembling or fading voice.* One common sign of stress is a dry sensation in the throat or a voice that just gives out at the end of the sentence. For the dry throat, take a sip of water and keep it nearby. If you are getting over a cold, you can get a little plastic dispenser with thin, dissolvable sheets of over the counter medication that will stave off a coughing jag (This is preferable to cough drops because it does not interfere with speech). Voices also tremble or give out because, when we are nervous, we tend to breathe in a very shallow, panting sort of way. Make a deliberate effort to breathe before you start talking and take deep breaths periodically. If you will be using a microphone, be certain to do a sound check before beginning. Pounding on the microphone and asking "Is this thing on?" or creating a loud screeching sound are not a good way to begin an important presentation.
4. *Perspiration.* If you get sweaty palms or a dripping forehead bring a small fabric handkerchief and discreetly blot the offending area. There products on the market to control excessive perspiration and odor. If the temperature of the room is an issue, see if someone who works at the facility can adjust the thermostat.
5. *Shaky hands.* The best way to conceal this sign of nervousness is to keep your fingers together or hold something (e.g., a small stack of papers) so that the trembling is not as obvious.
6. *Skin reactions.* Some people get pink splotches all over their necks or break out in hives before or during public speaking. Select clothing that will cover the

neck, chest, and arms, such as a long-sleeved turtleneck so that it is less obvious to the audience.

7. *An embarrassing mistake.* If you say the wrong word, just say, "Excuse me, what I meant to say was…" If something clumsy occurs, such as dropping or knocking over something or stumbling, just pause, smile knowingly to indicate that you realize it was an error, and move on without making too much of it.
8. *Technical difficulties.* Having problems with equipment is a scourge of presenters. Your best insurance is to always have more than one way to give the presentation. You could, for example, bring your own equipment and paper copies. It is much more frustrating to watch people try to solve a technical problem for 15 or 20 min than to just apologize and go to Plan B (or C).

For more on coping with anxiety during presentations, see the YouTube video by Deborah Grayson Riegel, Overcoming Nerves When Giving a Presentation. There are many more videos by experts on professional speakers posted here as well.

Memory Aids

A common concern of presenters is that they will forget what they have to say or lose their place while making the presentation. Try some of these strategies to prevent forgetting:

- Put the important points on small, numbered note cards. Remember that they are for your use only and do not need to make sense to anyone else. If you want to share an example, there's no need to write the whole story, just write EX and a word, phrase or sketch that will remind you.
- Use PowerPoint slides that contain the key phrases. Make sure that the slides aren't too cluttered and text-dense.
- Post an agenda or outline that shares the overview with your audience and keeps you on track.
- Create a graphic organizer that looks like a start to finish gameboard with words and pictures to guide your presentation.

Presentation Software

Who among us has not experienced the mind-numbing experience of watching a speaker read from a parade of PowerPoint slides? This situation is so common that it has been given the name of "death by PowerPoint" (Verderber et al. 2014). Whether it is PowerPoint or Prezi, the fault lies, not with the software, but with inappropriate use of the tool. Whatever presentation software you choose, slides should not be viewed as script for the unprepared or underprepared speaker. Instead, they are *talking* points (Daniels 2013). Presenters should be sufficiently well versed with their material to be able to conduct the session without slides. The purpose of the material on the slides is to jog the presenter's memory and to provide a concise, organized synopsis of the session.

Online Resources about PowerPoint Presentations

Oral Presentation and Powerpoint | Style for Students Online
https://www.e-education.psu.edu/styleforstudents/c7_p4.html
This Pennsylvania State University site gives students a crash course on how to use PowerPoint effectively.

How Can I Make My PowerPoint Presentations Amazing?—Lifehacker
http://lifehacker.com/how-can-i-make-my-powerpoint-presentations-amazing-507552122
This site delves into the details of producing an effective PowerPoint and links to examples of powerful speeches from TedTalks.

Johnson, L. K. (2011). Graphics dos and don'ts for PowerPoint. *Young Lawyer, 16* (3), 3.
Highlights what—and what not—to do with PPt.

Making a PowerPoint Presentation
www.iasted.org/conferences/formatting/presentations-tips.ppt
"Dos and don'ts" of PowerPoint–with examples.

Tips for Making Effective PowerPoint Presentations
http://www.ncsl.org/legislators-staff/legislative-staff/legislative-staff-coordinating-committee/tips-for-making-effective-powerpoint-presentations.aspx
The "Seven Deadly Sins" of PowerPoint and exceptionally detailed instructions on preparing better slides.

Fielding Questions

Novice presenters are sometimes particularly worried that someone will ask them a question and they will not know the answer. Some of this fear probably emanates from their lives as students when they were expected to supply the correct answer. The first step in handling this worry is to acknowledge that the most important questions often do not have facile answers. For instance, one of the leading experts on intelligence, Howard Gardner, was speaking at a conference when someone asked him, "Why did you identify seven distinctive types of human intelligence?

How did you arrive at that number?" In response, he humbly stated that, while the research suggested seven, there could be more—or fewer. There is no disgrace in admitting that you do not know the answer to a question or that there may not be a definitive answer. If an answer probably exists and you don't happen to know it, you can turn to your audience and request their expertise, ask someone to check it out online, or say that you'll investigate it further and share what you find.

Another important point about handling questions is to make sure that you understand the question. When in doubt, ask that the question be restated or clarified and answer that question directly, rather than talking more generally about a point of interest on which you are better prepared to speak.

Activity: Answering Questions Appropriately

Be certain that you are answering in a way implied by the question. For example:

- "What are some ways to…?" asks for different options, so list various possibilities rather than expounding on one.
- "Isn't this just another…?" suggests that there is nothing new here; clarify how what you are discussing represents a stride forward.
- "What if…?" asks for problem-solving; respond with practical solutions.
- "Why didn't you…?" asks for insight into how a decision was reached; give your rationale without being defensive.

It also is common to get a lengthy question that is more along the lines of a rather lengthy comment. Try to "read between the lines" before you respond. It is possible to respond without being dismissive, for example: "You bring up an interesting point and it's clear that you have given it considerable thought. I also happen to agree with you about….. Next question?" Sometimes, a question is so context-specific that it probably is not of great interest to the group. In this situation, you may want try something such as, "It sounds as though you have many questions that are particular to your situation but I'm not sure that I can address them adequately with the whole group in the time we have remaining. I'm going to suggest that we plan to talk when…" Then you can suggest a time, such as during the break, after the session, and so forth.

Hints on Handouts

Inexperienced presenters often go in search of materials produced by others that they can duplicate rather than developing their own resources. This is a mistake for several reasons. First of all, some materials may be protected by copyright. Second, it is rare to find the perfect match for a session and this leads to more copying than is necessary. Third, it sends the message that the speaker is not an expert and has to "borrow" someone else's expertise. Nevertheless, most participants want something in their hands to read, revisit, and carry back home. Some guidelines for handouts are:

- *Be selective.* It is not necessary to decimate a forest by making paper copies of mounds of materials.
- *Synthesize.* Participants will appreciate a best-evidence synthesis of research; for example, a table of major research findings is easier to process and more useful than many pages of text copied from different articles.
- *Proofread.* Any mistakes that are made on handouts will be pointed out by the participants and erode confidence in the presenter.
- *Determine how and when materials will be distributed.* They should not be distracting. For example, it probably will be better to distribute the PowerPoint after the session rather than before; otherwise, people may read through the entire session while waiting for the group to assemble and lose interest. Do let participants know that they will get a notes or outline copy of the slides so that they can give their full attention rather than taking notes. For an all-day session, you won't want to keep stopping to hand out papers and may want to create one or more packets of information.

Rebounding from a Disappointing Session

Before making a presentation, rely on planning and preparation rather than hopeful dreaming. For example, a presenter was invited to speak on adult literacy at an all-day institute and, during the introduction, mentioned that, on average, people in the United States read less than one book a year. Almost before that sentence was completed, a person's hand shot up and he asked, "I find that hard to believe. Where did you get that statistic?" Fortunately, the speaker had the citation, taken from an annual, national study conducted by the American Booksellers Association. She then added that it is estimated that 90 % of the book reading in the U.S. is accomplished by about 10 % of the population. She went on to explain that for those of us who are teachers, graduate students, and professors, it seems surprising that book reading is so infrequent but that this does not mean that other, shorter pieces of writing are not read. If the presenter had not been prepared, that question near the beginning of the session might have diminished her competence in the eyes of the group.

When we see great speakers, they give the mistaken impression that what they are doing is "natural". Therefore, one common mistake occurs when novices attempt to emulate expert presenters who make the task look deceptively easy. A group of four doctoral students from the English Department learned this through a disappointing experience. One of them asked, "How do you recover from a disastrous presentation?" and then went on to explain that, when they had watched their professors make a panel discussion the previous year at a major conference, it appeared to be very casual and unrehearsed. The contribution of each presenter flowed from one to the next. When they attempted this, however, things went horribly awry. They had not arrived at a meeting of the minds before the panel discussion and, as a result, the time was not managed well. In fact, one of the panelists who made the trip barely had a chance to speak before the time allocated for the session had elapsed. Several participants left the room as the session's disorganization became evident. The participants were harshly critical of what transpired on the session evaluations as well.

How can presenters "bounce back" from such disappointing results? The first step is to analyze what went wrong, exactly—in this case, the problem was inadequate planning. Doing this helps to step away from dwelling on what you could, should, or would have done and moves you into positive action mode. So, the panelists tried again but, this time, they produced a minute-by-minute script of what would occur at the session and who was responsible for each part. They appointed a time keeper and met to rehearse. They also developed some print materials to distribute to their participants. Nevertheless, they approached the session with some trepidation, still remembering on their negative experience during the previous year. This is when presenters have has to trust in their preparation and now that they genuinely did their best. The group of doctoral students was thrilled with the outcome the second time. In fact, one of the authors of their textbooks for a class attended and thanked them for an excellent presentation, saying that he would use the material they had distributed.

Conclusion

Sometimes, despite every effort, a presentation does not succeed. One professional consultant, for example, was invited to speak to all of the teachers from a large school district in Chicago. After the session began, she noticed that people appeared to be losing interest and that there were many whispered conversations going on. Then the superintendent announced that they were experiencing an unexpected, heavy snowfall and that everyone needed to get home before travel conditions worsened. Situations such as these are unavoidable. When things like this happen, remember the old English proverb: "A smooth sea never made a skilled mariner"—each time we present under less-than-ideal conditions, we can learn from it.

Online Resources for Improving as a Presenter

15 Recommendations for Designing and Delivering Effective Conference Presentations

http://www.facultyfocus.com/articles/faculty-development/15-recommendations-for-designing-and-delivering-effective-conference-presentations/

Prominent author/speaker Stephen Brookfield's advice to higher education faculty members.

How to Present Papers at Academic Conferences
www.editing.tw/download/SpeechD.ppt
This PPt offers a "crash course" on the entire presentation, from start to finish. The section on handling Q and A is especially helpful.

Belben, C. (2003). Making a gift of yourself: Preparing for successful conference presentations. *Teacher Librarian, 31*(1), 12–14.
Advice from a librarian on preparing to present.

Shane, B. (2012). A video recording and viewing protocol for student group presentations: Assisting self-assessment through a Wiki environment. *Computers and Education, 59*(3), 855–860.
Although this focuses on student presentations, the criteria for self-evaluation are helpful for presenters in various situations.

How to Prepare and Present a Conference Presentation
https://blogs.baruch.cuny.edu/cacophony/2010/10/13/how-to-prepare-and-present-a-conference-presentation/
City University of New York's Communications Department offers advice to beginners on making effective conference presentations.

References

Adler, L. (2015). Talking the talk: Tips on giving a successful conference presentation. Retrieved May 29, 2015 from http://www.apa.org/science/about/psa/2010/04/presentation.aspx.
American Evaluation Association. (2015). The art and science of a successful presentation: An annotated bibliography. Retrieved June 3, 2015 from http://files.archivists.org/conference/nola2013/Successful-Presentations.pdf.
Daniels, G. (2013). How to get your abstract accepted and how to present it. *ISBT Science Series, 9* (1), 51–55. doi:10.1111/voxs.12069.
Happell, B. (2009). Presenting with precision: Preparing and delivering a polished conference presentation. *Nurse Researcher, 16*(3), 45–56.
Sprague, J., Stuart, D., & Bodary, D. (2015). *The speaker's handbook* (11th ed.). Boston, MA: Cengage Learning.
Verderber, R., Sellnow, D., & Verderber, K. (2014). *The challenge of effective speaking in a digital age*. Boston, MA: Cengage Learning.

Part II
Types of Presentations

Section Overview

Universities expect graduate students and faculty to have active research agendas. The term "active agenda" is defined differently by different institutions. This section begins with a definition of the term "research" and a description of the range of scholarly endeavors that can be described as research. We then describe how you can identify a conference, gain a working knowledge of the different sessions offered, and reflect on your scholarship before making a decision. Given that some sessions place greater demand on a beginning scholar than others, the sessions described here have been sequenced from basic to advanced. Graduate students and beginning scholars should plan to work their way down the list during their professional career. Mid-career faculty who may have already gained expertise with some should consider assuming leadership positions; for example, serving as chair and/or discussant, volunteering to serve as conference organizer and/or keynote speaker.

Dunn, Pryor, and Yates (2005) define research as "not just a question of what is considered, but how it is done" (p. 175). They go on to add that "the interaction between substantive and methodological issues means, therefore, that both the content and the methodology are dynamic, involving constant shifting" (p. 175). The word "research" encompasses many different types of scholarly endeavors. Murray (2013) lists the following types in her book *Writing for Academic Journals:*

- Data-driven papers such as meta-study papers, artifact papers, work-in-progress papers.
- Method papers such as method introductions, tutorial papers, method mongering, demonstration of a concept.
- Theoretical papers introducing a new theory, explaining someone else's theory, refining or extending theory, critiquing existing theory, setting the agenda for a needed new theory.

- Consciousness-raising papers pointing to issues often ignored, applying methods that are established in another field.
- Perspective papers showing what it is and how it affects research and knowledge.
- Agenda setting papers.
- Review papers.
- Position papers.

The value that different conferences place on each of the above may vary across disciplines. Therefore, the decision about where to present should be given careful thought.

Step 1: Identifying a Conference

Research universities expect faculty to present at several national and international conference presentations a year. Presenters can initially start with two, one in fall and one in spring or summer. The web sites listed in Box 1 can be used as a starting point. The initial list of possible conferences that you develop should include both discipline- and content-specific national and international conferences. This list can be refined further in consultation with departmental colleagues.

Box 1 Web sites that List Upcoming Conferences

1. AllConferences.com (http://www.allconferences.com)
2. ConferenceRegistry.com (http://www.conferenceregistry.com)
3. Conal Conference Alerts (http://www.conferencealerts.com)
4. Conferensum (http://www.conferensum.com)
5. Teaching Conferences Directory (http://cetl.kennesaw.edu/teaching-conferences-directory) published by the Center for Excellence in Teaching and Learning at Kennesaw State University in Georgia.

It is important that the conferences align not only with your research interests but also with your schedule. Given that major conferences set the dates for next year's conference well in advance, it is possible to keep those dates free of other commitments. It is also important to keep track of when calls for conference papers are released and submission deadlines are announced. Larger conferences release their call for proposals six to ten months beforehand. Consider adding your name to conference listservs to receive conference updates promptly. Presenters can greatly improve their ability to get on the conference program if they access the call and begin the planning process well before the deadline.

Step 2: Gaining a Working Knowledge of Different Sessions

Each conference session has very unique features. Presenters need to gain working knowledge of the different types of sessions that are possible before identifying one that best fits their immediate professional needs and long-term career goals. Figure 1 illustrates the different types of sessions offered by a large majority of conferences, organized in terms of scope and organization.

1. *Large group sessions.* These include workshops and professional development sessions which are typically assigned a room of their own. Professionals who have had considerable experience on the other side of the podium should consider sharing their expertise through workshops. A keynote address is often an invited session, often in the largest room at a conference venue. Accomplished scholars who have earned name recognition can position themselves to be invited as a keynote speaker.
2. *Concurrent sessions.* Poster and roundtable sessions, which are often grouped thematically, are offered concurrently in large conference rooms. Both are free-flowing and informal in nature. At poster sessions, the attendees move to any part of the room to engage presenters in a conversation. Likewise, at roundtable sessions, attendees join a table, listen to each presentation, and then engage in dialogue with the presenters at that table. Paper sessions are offered concurrently in smaller rooms. Each paper session, organized thematically by conference organizers, typically includes 3–5 papers that are presented sequentially. The session concludes with a discussion led by the discussant or chair.
3. *Thematic concurrent sessions.* These include symposia and/or panel discussions, and working group roundtables. They are grouped, not by the conference organizers, but by the presenters themselves. They provide attendees to with an opportunity to participate in the examination of a topic, problem, or theme, from a variety of perspectives with groups of individuals who were involved in different projects.

Presenters should read the conference call for proposals very carefully to determine if some types of papers are preferred over others. For example, some divisions of a professional association may accept only empirical papers while others accept conceptual and theoretical papers as well. Conferences like the National Association for the Education of Young Children (NAEYC) and the National Association for Multicultural Education (NAME) list sessions by duration instead of session type (see Box 2). This approach provides conference presenters with the freedom to choose any of the sessions listed in Fig. 1 within the chosen time frame.

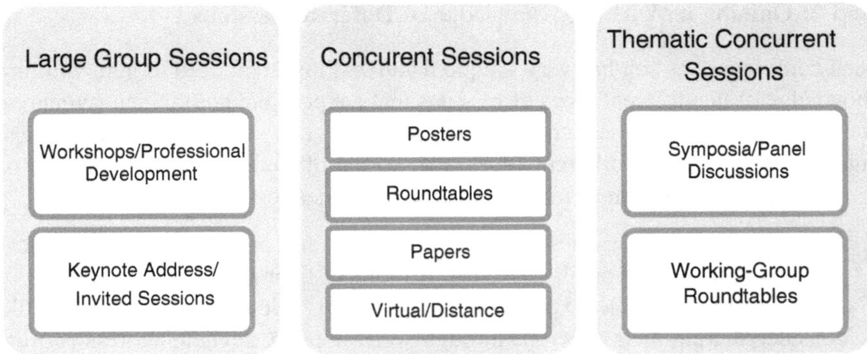

Fig. 1 Conference Sessions by Scope and Organization

Box 2 Excerpt from a Call for Proposals Presenters can submit proposals for one-hour, two-hour, or research poster sessions.

1. One-hour sessions are forums for information dissemination—including sessions that address current issues, present recent research findings, provide an overview of proposed legislation, and such. They can include questions from the floor.
2. Two- hour sessions include participant interaction during ***at least half*** of the scheduled time. Participants have opportunities to engage in discussions with colleagues, reflect on session content, and consider ways to implement what they have learned.
3. Research poster sessions present cutting-edge research in the field of early childhood education. Institute participants can review the poster displays and discuss the research methodology and findings with researchers.

Source http://www.naeyc.org/institute/2015-call-presentation-proposals

Another way to gain a working knowledge of different types of conference presentations is to access resources provided by professional organizations on their web site. For example, the AERA Graduate Student Council's repository includes successful proposals across the eight divisions and reviewers' comments. To access these example proposals visit http://www.aera.net/AboutAERA/MemberConstituents/GraduateStudentCouncil/GSCProposalTipsExamples/tabid/15440/Default.aspx

Step 3: Reflecting on Scholarship The decision about how to present your scholarship to fellow professionals in the field merits careful consideration and action. Presenters need to carefully consider the purpose of their presentation as well as how far along they are in terms of completion. Informal sessions like roundtables and poster sessions would be more beneficial to presenters exploring new ideas. The feedback received on work in progress can be used to shape a study, validate instruments, and/ or refine analytic procedures. Presenters who have completed a study but have not started developing the manuscript could also present their work as a roundtable or poster. The feedback from others offers a form of peer review that may be helpful when developing the manuscript. Projects that are near completion and well into the manuscript preparation phase would be better suited to paper presentations, symposia, and working roundtables. In addition to receiving critique, both from the discussant as well as attendees, presenters may receive an invitation from editors who attend the session to submit the completed manuscript to their journals. Symposia and working roundtables will connect presenters with like-minded scholars involved in projects with greater scope.

Another important consideration is your current position in the tenure and promotion process. Informal presentations, such as roundtables and posters at local and national conferences are generally more acceptable during the earlier years. With each passing year, the expectations for paper presentations at national and international venues tend to escalate. In addition, there may be an expectation for single-authored work in order for faculty members to advance professionally in some departments and disciplines. Presenters would benefit greatly from informal conversations with colleagues to unpack unwritten departmental rules about what constitutes an acceptable level of scholarly activity at each career phase.

Chapter 4
Workshop/Professional Development Sessions

One common type of conference presentation is a one-hour workshop/professional development training session. Such sessions provide attendees with an opportunity to engage in a series of hands-on activities led by a content area expert. They illustrate key concepts, recommended strategies, and successful practices based on synthesis of theory/research.

Scope

Workshops/professional development sessions tend to be popular with professionals at different stages of their careers. Using an interactive approach, presenters engage participants in activities that relate to a common problem, project, or shared interest. The activities selected need to support meaningful interaction, discussion, and reflection.

Format

At larger conferences workshop/professional development sessions are sometimes offered the day before the conference begins or as a separate strand throughout the conference. At smaller, practitioner-oriented conferences, workshops tend to predominate. Workshops/professional development sessions may be led by one or more presenters and usually, the audience size is approximately 20–30 people. These sessions could be scheduled to last anywhere between 1–6 h, although a one-hour session is the most common. Attendees are occasionally encouraged to bring their laptops with them so that they can participate more actively in sessions.

M.R. Jalongo and C. Machado, *Making Effective Presentations at Professional Conferences*, SpringerBriefs in Education,
DOI 10.1007/978-3-319-23174-7_4

How to Propose a Workshop

Expectations for workshops/trainings vary from conference to conference. Some conferences, such as the American Educational Research Association (AERA), require that proposals relate to the research process or other areas of research professionals' work (e.g., obtaining research funding, serving as a peer reviewer, presenting research to public audiences, integrating diverse theories, using a particular research method or technique). Other conferences encourage workshop presenters to focus on skills development and provide participants with hands-on experience.

Workshop proposals are often brief. Presenters typically are required include the following information in a proposal.

- A clear, concise title
- A 150–200-word abstract that is later included in the conference program
- A brief description of the intended audience (experience level and prerequisites)
- The proposed length (1, 2, 3 or 6 h)
- A list of three to five concise, clearly articulated learning objectives or outcomes for the participants
- A detailed agenda or plan for content delivery
- A summary of the workshop/professional development presenters' qualifications.

Some conferences employ an anonymous peer-review process for workshops/professional development sessions while others require presenters to identify themselves and explain the contribution of the session to the overall conference program.

Workshop/professional development titles should be crafted very carefully. As evident from the two examples presented in Box 4.1, titles should capture, in 10 words or less, the topic that will be covered and, if appropriate, the intended audience. The titles presented below include key words that evoke curiosity and set expectations for the session. A well written title can help prevent the presenter from straying too far from the purpose and/or argument (Murray 2013). Abstracts should build on the title. A well written abstract clearly communicates: (1) what attendees will take away from the presentation, (2) the specific content to be delivered, (3) the type of delivery methods used to convey the information, and (4) the benefits for attendees. Presenters should carefully ensure that the detailed agenda of the workshop actually delivers all that is promised in the title and abstract.

Box 4.1. Sample Workshop Abstracts
Singing and Signs
Authors and Conference: Lindsay Barnhart, Lecturer, University of Wisconsin-Stout, Early Childhood Conference, 2015

Singing and the use of sign language (ASL) are two amazing tools. Put them together for a high level of student engagement and learning.

Participants will actively participate in learning signs to infant/toddler and preschool appropriate songs. (Infant/toddler, Preschool)

Source: http://www.uwstout.edu/profed/ece/ececonf/conf_workshops.cfm

Differentiating Instruction: Meeting the Needs of All Learners with MOOCs

Author and Conference: Jamie Brandon, Carnegie Mellon; Crystal Machado, Indiana University of Pennsylvania, Lilly Conference 2015

Massive Open Online Courses (MOOCs) that enrol thousands of students across the globe are viewed by some as a threat and others as a way to solve critical higher education issues. The presenters will provide an overview of the types of MOOCs and popular platforms through which they are offered. Taking a social justice perspective, the presenters will describe how the needs of overlooked populations can be met by differentiating instruction across content, process, and product.

The terms "learning objectives" and "learning outcomes" are often used interchangeably. The former is expressed from the perspective of the presenters' performance, the latter from the students' performance. Listed below is an example of each:

- Example of a Learning Objective: The presenter will model the use of structured discovery and then engage participants in a discussion.
- Example of a Learning Outcome: Attendees will list three of the benefits of using structured discovery after participating in a hands-on activity.

Jalongo (2013) recommends that presenters who are new to writing conference proposals should begin with the minute-by-minute agenda or plan for content delivery (see Chap. 3). A workshop/professional development proposal should allocate time appropriately. Carter and Curtis (2002) offer a very useful structure for the typical, one-hour session.

- Welcome, introductions, overview (5–10 min.)
- Opening activity to reflect on topic (10 min.)
- Presentation of core ideas (10–15 min.)
- Practice applying ideas (15–20 min.)
- Next steps and follow-up (5–10 min).
- Summary and evaluation (5 min.)

Another way of organizing the session is to take an "I do", "We do", and "You do" approach. This works particularly well when teaching a practical skill, such as learning a technology skill. The cycle implies that the presenter first demonstrates with examples. Then the group works together to produce a product. Finally, each participant applies what she or he has learned to produce an example. Box 4.2 suggests a way to think through a workshop by focusing on what the participants will do. If co-presenting, presenters can make a schedule that indicates who is doing which parts.

Box 4.2 Agenda/Plan for Content Delivery for a Workshop/Professional Development Session
Title of Workshop: Planning Instructional Internationalizing Efforts

- Current Efforts—Ask participants to share what their institutions currently do to plan internationalization efforts
- Increasing Efforts—Invite participants to brainstorm stakeholders and necessary messages needed to rally support for planning internationalization efforts
- Drafting Messages—Create small groups, focusing on a specific stakeholder in your institution; draft communications recruiting this group to be involved
- Planning Next Steps—Review the content introduced and ask participants to decide how they might use this new material when they return home

Source: http://www.nafsa.org/Attend_Events/Annual_Conference/Presenting_And_Training_Guide/Session_or_Workshop_Design/

In many ways, the all-day session is an expanded version of the one-hour workshop; both rely on learner engagement and skill development in order to be effective. Some examples of these longer sessions are: in-service trainings for professionals supported by employers, pre-conference institutes that are offered on the day before the general conference begins, and "conference within a conference" all day sessions that focus on the interests of a particular group. For example, the National Association of Early Childhood Teacher Educators—the college/university faculty members responsible for preparing the next generation of teachers—hosts a conference embedded in the more general organization, the National Association for the Education of Young Children. Likewise, some of the groups that accredit college-level programs conduct all day sessions for university faculty at professional conferences.

In order to maximize the effectiveness of the time that presenters spend with participants, some conference planners are implementing a different strategy. Instead of the presenter devoting much of the time to building background, just the reverse occurs: attendees are provided with many resources in advance and arrive with the necessary background already built. That way, when the group meets, it is a more interactive experience that emphasizes collaboration and networking (Yensen 2013). The concept of a "flipped presentation" is borrowed from the flipped classroom in which students are expected to complete a variety of activities prior to (rather than during) the session itself.

Online Resources for Workshop/Professional Development Sessions

Designing and Delivering a Training Session and Workshop
http://ctb.ku.edu/en/table-of-contents/structure/training-and-technical-assistance/design-training-session/main
This University of Kansas site offers information on how to design and deliver a training, checklists to guide planning, tools for evaluation, and PowerPoints to summarize.

Planning a Workshop
http://www.mindtools.com/pages/article/PlanningAWorkshop.htm
Strategies for increasing interactivity links to information about the role of a facilitator, ice breaker ideas, and tips for organizing team decision making are available at this site.

How to Conduct a Workshop
http://www.wikihow.com/Conduct-a-Workshop
This collaboratively written how-to guide lists eight strategies that aid in planning for, delivering, and evaluating a workshop.

Checklist for Workshop/Professional Development Sessions

Before the Workshop/Professional Development Session

- Visit the conference website to get a sense of what the room will be like and the technology available. This information could influence your choice of activities.
- Print out a copy of the names of attendees who have registered for the session. If you do not have access to this information you can contact a conference organizer. Additionallly, prepare a sign-up sheet to keep track of all who ultimately attend. Include a column for them to add their email addresses and institutional affiliations.
- Assess your audience's level of familiarity with the material in advance, if possible. For example, when a professor was asked to conduct a workshop on journal writing for teachers at their professional development day, she asked to speak to a few of them beforehand to gauge their level of experience with students' journal writing. By doing this, she could do a better job of tailoring the session to the group's needs.
- Prepare presentation material. In addition to the content, include a cover page with the title of the workshop, the date, your contact information and a machine-readable code, also called a QR code, which makes it easier to store urls on smart phones. The QR code will make it possible for attendees to access your material digitally.

- Create handouts that include thought-provoking questions and/or data that you can use to engage participants in higher-order thinking. Include the date and your email address in the footer so that conference attendees can contact you for permission, at a later date, if they wish to reuse the material. Take at least 10–15 extra handouts.
- Save your presentation material and handouts on a flash drive and/or in the cloud if you use Google Drive or Dropbox. so you can access your material if your laptop fails to function.
- Take business cards to share with attendees who might like to contact you later.

During the Workshop/Professional Development Session

- Finish setting up the room at least 10 min before the session is scheduled to begin. Organize the furniture in the room in a manner that facilitates smooth transition from one activity to the next. Place the sign in sheet and handouts near the entrance of the room for easy access.
- Mingle informally with attendees who show up early.
- Position yourself near the entrance of the room 5 min before the session begins and welcome attendees.
- Quickly assess attendees' level of familiarity with material with a "show of hands survey" (e.g., "How many of you have experience conducting focus group interviews?").
- Listen attentively to conversations that take place during small group discussions. This will make it easier for you to tailor your comments to attendees' needs during whole group discussions.
- Manage time appropriately. You might bring a watch or small clock, ask a co-presenter to keep time, or use with a cell phone application that keeps time.

After a Workshop and Professional Development Session

- Chat with attendees as they prepare to leave the room. Give them your business card, if requested.
- Approach attendees who showed a special interest in the session and inquire about the work they have done in this area. This interaction could lead to future partnerships.
- Keep a record of all questions and comments from attendees for future reference. This can be particularly helpful if you decide to present the session again or develop an article from the presentation.
- Send an email to attendees the day after the session to thank them for their participation and let them know you would be willing to assist them in the future. If the workshop was excellent, this interaction could result in an invited workshop at their institutions.

References

Carter, M., & Curtis, D. (2002). *Training teachers: A harvest of theory and practice*. St. Paul, MN: Redleaf Press.

Jalongo, M. R. (2013). Getting on the conference program and writing a practical article: Templates for success. *Early Childhood Education Journal, 41*, 13–23.

Murray, R. (2013). *Writing for academic journals*. Boston, MA: Pearson.

Yesen, J. (2013). Flipped presentations for effective conferencing. Retrieved May 27, 2015 from ojni.org/issues/?p=2390.

Zelazny, G. (2000). *Say it with presentations: How to design and deliver successful business presentations*. New York, NY: McGraw-Hill.

Chapter 5
Roundtable Sessions

A roundtable discussion at a conference often, quite literally, is professional dialogue that takes place at a round table surrounded by 6–10 chairs. Each table is numbered and additional chairs are available around the room to be added to popular roundtable discussions.

Scope

Roundtable sessions tend to be popular with professionals at different stages of their careers. During these informal sessions, presenters describe works-in-progress that may be at the design, implementation, data collection, data analysis and/or manuscript preparation phase. At large conferences, it is not unusual for these sessions to be scheduled for a room large enough to accommodate as many as 10–30 roundtable sessions concurrently. The session could last anywhere between 60–90 min. Presenters can use the feedback to develop their idea, research questions, instrument, analytic approach etc.

Format

At some conferences, roundtable sessions are nonthematic while at others, they are organized by theme. For thematic roundtables, each session includes four or five papers that are interrelated in some way. For example, the American Educational Research (AERA) conference in 2014 included a roundtable session titled: *A Global Examination of Teacher Preparation*. The papers in this session included a comparative analysis of English as a foreign language programs in Turkey and USA; a comparative analysis of K-12 and adult educator study programs in Germany, a paper that described knowledge building and identity development

M.R. Jalongo and C. Machado, *Making Effective Presentations at Professional Conferences*, SpringerBriefs in Education,
DOI 10.1007/978-3-319-23174-7_5

processes of literacy educators; and a paper that discussed the characteristics of teacher preparation programs that predict early career teacher preparedness.

The presenters of four to five papers and session chair are typically assigned a table at which the informal discussion takes place. Approximately three to five attendees may choose to join a roundtable and participate in the discussion. The chair introduces the session and the presenters, manages time, and facilitates the discussion. Depending upon the number of presenters per session, each presenter is given approximately 8–10 min to present their paper. Additionally, presenters are given approximately 5 min to respond to questions, either immediately after their presentation, or at the end, following oral delivery of all papers included in that session. Other conventions may be followed by conferences. At some conferences roundtables include papers related to different topics. Presenters may be expected to run the session without the assistance of an assigned chair.

Presenters typically are expected to provide a one-page hand-out and/or a copy of their presentation material which includes their contact information. Technologically savvy presenters have begun to include a QR code on the first page of their presentation material; this makes it possible for attendees to access the material digitally with their smartphone. It also makes it easier for attendees to establish contact with presenters after the conference.

How to Propose a Roundtable

Depending upon the popularity and selectivity of the conference presenters may be asked to submit either an abstract (see Box 5.1) or a one to three page description of the study. In addition to abstract, longer proposals typically includes the following elements:

- Title
- Research Problem
- Purpose of the Study
- Research Questions
- Significance of the Study
- Methodology (data sources and data collection procedures)
- Results/Findings/Description of Feedback Needed

Box 5.1 Sample Abstract for a Roundtable Session
Title: The "American Educational Experience" in a Predominantly White Rural Community as Described by International Students: An Opportunity to Redefine Priorities
Authors: Crystal Machado and Jason A. Smith, Indiana University of Pennsylvania

Roundtable Session: International Undergraduate Students in Higher Education

Abstract: Current research suggests that international students should bear the responsibility of integrating into host societies. Few studies recognize that purposeful or inadvertent marginalization could be occurring. Typological and interpretive analysis of data generated through interviews with 14 international students at a research university in a predominantly white rural community allowed researchers to identify zones of tolerance on and off campus. This paper will provide a thematic analysis relating to challenges faced in the community, where many of the intolerant acts were experienced. Findings suggest a need for evaluative research and innovative culturally responsive programming that acknowledges the existence of structural inequality and overturns parochialism on campuses and in communities.

Box 5.2 presents an abbreviated version of a roundtable proposed by Fife Demski and presented at the AERA 2014 conference in Philadelphia. The example illustrates the importance of using both theoretical and empirical research to contextualize the study and establish a need for it. The research questions are clear, concise, and explore different facets of the purpose statement. It is evident, from the description of procedures, that the author used a rigorous approach to collect data over an extended period of time.

Box 5.2 Excerpt from a Roundtable Proposal: Research Problem, Purpose of the Study and Research Questions and Data Collection Procedures

Title: Negotiating Fears: White Student Teachers Immersed in a Diverse Urban Setting

Authors: Veronica Marie Fife-Demski, Ball State University

Roundtable Session: Field Experiences for Pre-service Urban Teachers' Learning and Development.

Research Problem: Nearly 29 % of teachers leave public schools within their first year (Ingersoll & Merrill 2010), and as many as 50 % of teachers leave the profession within their first 5 years of teaching. This particular statistic fails to mention that most new teachers find urban public schools even more challenging than public schools located in suburban neighborhoods. More often than not, urban public schools have less desirable working conditions, lower pay, unsupportive administrators, and a lack of basic resources. These challenges often lead to what Kozol (1991) has called "savage inequalities." Along with these obstacles, many urban schools are at risk, and are sometimes advocated (Smarick 2010) for being shut down. Furthermore, Ingersoll and Merrill (2010) have claimed, "data show a significant annual shuffling of teachers from poor to wealthier schools, from high-minority to low-minority schools, and from urban to suburban schools" (p. 19).

Specifically addressing new teachers and attrition rates, DeAngelis' and Presley (2011) found evidence of "new teacher attrition rates and student characteristics indicates that rates tend to be higher for teachers who begin their careers in schools with higher percentages of low-income, minority, and/or low-performing students" (p. 601). If beginning teachers are to be successful in urban schools, and in particular, beginning teachers that are not from urban areas, then preparation surely is key. A key aspect of becoming a successful urban teacher is learning to understand that pupils' community lives play an important role in their schooling (Brown 2003; Delpit 1995; Ladson-Billings 1994).

Purpose of the Study and Research Questions: The purpose of this study was to explore the struggles and challenges of Urban Student Teachers (USTs) and their experiences while attempting to cross cultural borders into school neighborhood communities through an immersive Urban Student Teaching Program (USTP). The following questions guided the research:

1. What did USTs experience during their student teaching semester in urban schools?
2. What struggles and challenges did USTs experience during their attempts to become border crossers as community members and teachers in urban neighborhoods and schools?

Data Collection Procedures: The USTP requires year-long preparatory coursework, as well as continued coursework during the sixteen-week student teaching placement. Data collection included: interviews, observations, serendipitous experiences, and document reviews. The five informants were interviewed five times throughout their student teaching semester. They were interviewed before they began their student teaching semester in order to gain insight on their expectations, as well as at the conclusion of their experience in order to gain insight of their overall experience. They were observed three times within their classrooms during the beginning, middle, and end of their sixteen-week placement. Interviews followed each observation. Interviews covered questions concerning teaching, as well as community immersion. The USTs were additionally observed during serendipitous experiences, such as community meetings. All documents were reviewed from the year and a half program involvement.

Box 5.3 includes excerpts from a roundtable session proposed by Wen, Jiang and Machado and presented at the New England Education Research Association (NEERO) conference. Box 5.4 includes excerpts from the results and conclusion section of the roundtable session proposed by Peterson, Gibbons and Singleton and presented at the AERA 2014 conference.

Box 5.3 Excerpt from a Roundtable Proposal: Purpose of the Study, Data Collection and Analysis, Timeline and Feedback Anticipated
Title: Promise or Peril? Effects of Digital Writing on College Students' Formal Writing
Authors: Huachuan Wen, Kansas State University; Ying Jiang and Crystal Machado, Indiana University of Pennsylvania
Roundtable Session: Research in Progress

Purposes of the Study: This paper will describe the theoretical framework, research design and preliminary findings of a mixed method study that will be conducted in Spring 2012. The study explores the perceptions of college students, who might be a typical age group representing the "digital youth." The study will investigate how undergraduate students enrolled in college writing courses and their instructors perceive that their formal writing, i.e. writing for academic purposes, is affected by their digital writing.

Data Collection and Analysis: The author will send email invitations to all 44 instructors who are assigned to teach ENGL202 in Spring 2012. The first ten to respond will be included in the study. The instructors will administer the survey to their students in a computer lab in February 2012. Following preliminary analysis of the survey data the researchers will schedule interviews with the instructors. SPSS, quantitative research software, and Nvivo, qualitative research software will be used to analyze the data.

Timeline: Development of the survey instruments is currently underway. Following this, the survey and interview protocol will be validated. In November 2011 the researchers will go through the IRB application process. Data collection will begin in February 2012. The online survey will be administered in February 2012. Interviews will be conducted in March 2012. Data analysis will take place in April and May 2012. It is anticipated that the study will be completed by the time of presentation at this conference.

Feedback Anticipated: The design of the study and preliminary findings will be shared with the roundtable attendees. The presenters will elicit feedback about (a) the effectiveness of the data analysis approaches that were used (b) the clarity of the charts and tables that have been developed (c) possible publication avenues and (d) future research that can be designed in this area.

Box 5.4: Except from a Roundtable Proposal: Results and Conclusion
Title: Profession Driven: Teachers' Genres of Participation in Social Media Purpose
Authors: Margaret Polizos Peterson, Thor Gibbons and Elizabeth Singleton, University of Maryland—College Park

Roundtable Session: Technology in the Lives of Teachers

Results: In order to construct a nuanced understanding of the ways in which participants conceive and create communities of practice through social media, we approached the data initially coding for Wenger's (2000) conceptualization of community dimensions of *community, identity,* and *boundaries*. In addition, we employed Ito et al.'s framework for coding genres of participation as *interest-driven* or *friendship-driven.* Throughout our analyzing of the data, emic themes developed within participants' discourse surrounding their experiences with social media for collaboration and connection in the summer institute. By employing Charmaz's (2006) approach to constant-comparative analysis of emerging themes within the data, we discerned themes suggesting a fully *profession-driven genre of participation*.

RQ 1: We examined participants' discourse about and through social media through dimensions of communities of practice: (1) community, (2) boundaries, and (3) identity. Results suggest participants did construct a community of practice through use of social media by linking multiple communities and using the M-AUWP site as a hub to broker, build bridges, span, and expand their professional learning networks.

An example of how participants constructed a community of practice and utilized the affordances of social media to connect and maintain this nascent community is evident in participants' use of Twitter. While activity on the Facebook page took place off-site, apart from actual meetings of the Summer Institute, there were occasions during on-site meetings that participants used Twitter to create a back channel. This spontaneous web-supported conversation occurred simultaneously with a live presentation on making digital stories, for the purpose of processing learning and reflecting on future applications.

> Erin: Can't wait to make digital movies with my students next year! #M-AUWP
>
> Sarah: Teachers and students working together, learning together, in unfamiliar digital space. Multi-layered modeling, practice. #M-AUWP
>
> Thor: @blkdrama Thanks to Bonnie for sharing her and her students' digital pieces. I see the space of play in designing multimodal texts.

These "tweets" affirmed the value of the presentation as a source of community learning while suggesting the significance educational technology plays as a shared purpose for engaging with community.

Conclusions: Through the dimensions of *mutual engagement, joint enterprise, and shared repertoire*, the members of the M-AUWP used the social media spaces for profession-driven genres of participation. They "liked" each other's ideas, helped each other address gaps in the group's knowledge, and shared; curated and crafted original content around the group's identified topics of interest: teacher practice, technology integration, and educational activism. Through these profession-driven genres of participation, they developed relationships with one another as well as with experts from outside the community, negotiated new learning, and traversed a continuum as consumers and producers of content; these genres helped to develop their shared practice within a social learning system.

In this way, M-AUWP acted as a *community of practice*, where members met with multi-memberships intact, where interest-driven participation was allowed within the larger umbrella of a profession-driven social learning system. The interaction became a place, where professional development happened through exposure to and sharing of ideas with others in the community also engaged in teaching and learning, technology and/or activism. Further, the conception of true professional development was articulated by participants as one of collaboration, co-responsibility to the members of their learning community and a diversity of identities supported within all, some, or one of the interest-driven groups we discerned within this M-AUWP. Each of these profession-driven groups shared the goal of better development as professional educators, although they may have approached this goal in differing ways.

Wen et al.'s proposal is an example of work in process, they provide a timeline and describe the feedback they would like to receive from session attendees. Peterson et al. on the other hand present a discussion that relates the findings back to the theory. By including illustrative quotes they make it possible for the reader to evaluate the validity of findings. Conclusions have to be written very carefully. Peterson et al. relate their conclusions to the purpose of the study and results that were discussed earlier. Presenters of quantitative and mixed-method studies that are complete or near completion should describe their choice of instrument, include results in data tables, and discuss key findings explicitly in their proposals.

The roundtable sessions described above should not be confused with working group roundtable sessions. Working group sessions (see Fig. 5.1) allow attendees who are affiliated with different institutions to engage in synergistic discussions that begin at the session, continue beyond the conference and lead to mutually beneficial collaborative projects that extend the research agenda of members of the group.

Online Resources for Roundtable Sessions

SIOP Presentation Suggestions for Roundtable Sessions

http://www.siop.org/conferences/05Con/Presenters/Rountable.aspx

In addition to listing strategies for effective presentation this resource highlights some of the ways in which presenters can meet the needs of attendees with disabilities.

Role of the Facilitator

Armed with an agenda for the session, rather than scholarly papers, the chair/session organizer engages attendees in small group discussions that could focus on a single topic or multiple topics of interest. The chair, who is often the session organizer, welcomes co-presenters or invited facilitators 10 min before the session begins and helps them establish a reasonable comfort level with the room arrangement, technology, sequence of presentation and time limitations. The chair calls the session to order at the scheduled time, introduces the session and the co-presenters and/or invited facilitators, manages time, and ensures that the session schedule is followed. To facilitate a substantive exchange and interaction in small groups, different topics are assigned to each roundtable. Attendees are encouraged to pick a topic and engage in a discussion with other attendees seated at that table. For example, if a session is about starting a student-led journal, attendees can be divided into the following (1) the peer-review process (2) organization, management and funding, and (3) publication and marketing. The 15–20 min discussion at each table can be led by a co-presenter or invited guest who is knowledgeable about the content area. In this case, the discussion at each table could be led by editors of student-led journals or students who are actively engaged in managing student-led journals. Attendees have the opportunity to ask questions and contribute ideas. If appropriate, these are recorded and shared with subsequent groups that join the table to move the conversation forward. The ideas, questions or action items generated by each group can serve as agenda items for subsequent meetings and/or fodder for discussion in an online forum, which could be a blog, wiki, a shared Google document, or Facebook group.

How to Propose a Working-Group Roundtable Session

Working-group roundtable sessions are generally chosen based on the timeliness of the topic, originality, as well as the potential to engage attendees in an informative and synergistic discussion. Proposals generally include the following elements:

• A clear, concise title
• A 150–200-word abstract that is later included in the conference program
A brief description of the intended audience (experience level and prerequisites)
• The proposed length of session (1–2 h)
• A list of three to five concise, clearly articulated learning objectives or outcomes
• A detailed agenda or plan for content delivery
• A summary of working-group roundtable facilitators' and invited guests' qualifications.

Some conferences employ a blind peer-review process for such sessions; others require presenters to identify themselves so that they can evaluate presenters' qualifications and their contribution to the overall conference program.

Fig. 5.1 Working group roundtable sessions

How to Lead an Effective Roundtable Discussion
http://daralainemurray.com/2013/03/22/how-to-lead-an-effective-roundtable-discussion/
The author of this blog describes how attendees can be actively engaged in a discussion.

4 Tips for Planning and Hosting a Successful Roundtable
http://www.eventmanagerblog.com/organising-successful-roundtables
The author of this blog post emphasizes the importance of a clear focus, a comprehensive agenda, a strong moderator, and selective invites.

Checklist for Roundtable Sessions

Before the Roundtable Session

- Print a copy of the session as described in the conference program and/or the conference website. This will make it possible for you to identify and address the chair and other presenters by name when when you introduce yourself to them.
- Prepare presentation materials. This could include the paper itself, a one-page handout that summarizes the paper, a document that includes charts and tables that you hope to discuss with particpants, and/or a data collection instrument that you wish to share with attendees. In addition to the content include a cover page with the title of the workshop, the date, your contact information and a QR code on the first slide. The QR code will make it possible for attendees to access your material digitally and contact you later if they wish to reuse the material.
- Take at least 15 copies of handouts so you have enough for co-authors and anyone else who joins the roundtable session.
- If you intend to display information electronically you should bring your own laptop. The battery should be charged because you may not be located near a power outlet.
- If you plan to use digital techology like a PowerPoint, Prezi, or a Pinterest board to support content delivery save a copy on your laptop and on a storage device in case you do not have access to the internet. Be aware that some hotels charge very high fees for internet access in conference rooms.
- Save your presentation material and handouts on a flash drive and/or in the cloud if you use Google Drive or Dropbox so you can access your material if your laptop fails to function.
- Take business cards to share with attendees who might like to contact you later.

During the Roundtable Session

- Use the session number or title of the roundtable session to identify your table at least 10 min before it is scheduled to start.

- Introduce yourself to the chair and other presenters who are seated at the table and converse with them informally until the chair calls the session to order.
- Listen attentively to other presenters and take notes so that you can contribute more meaningfully when the discussion ensues.
- Manage your presentation time appropriately either with the assistance of the chair or with a cell phone application that keeps time.
- Distribute your one-page handout to everyone who is seated at the table just before you begin your presentation. Use it meaningfully and direct participants' attention to interesting trends and patterns in the data. Indicate very explictly the nature of the feedback you would like to receive.
- Keep a record of all questions and comments from attendees for future reference.

After the Roundtable Session

- Approach attendees who showed a special interest in your topic and inquire about the work they have done in this area.
- Chat with other presenters, the chair, and attendees as they prepare to leave. Give them your business card, if requested.
- Thank the chair personally at the end of the session, or later by email.
- Keep a record of all questions and comments from attendees for future reference.
- Send an email to attendees who contributed ideas or information that you intend to use to refine your manuscript. This interaction could lead to a co-authored presentation or publication.

Chapter 6
Poster Sessions

Poster sessions rely on a clear, concise, visually appealing, and professionally prepared display that captures the essence of a research project. Most of the time, those who present poster sessions are limited to a tri-fold display board, therefore, the challenge here is to represent ideas in a succinct, yet informative way using a visually appealing format.

Scope

Poster sessions tend to be more popular with graduate students and newer faculty. They provide presenters with an opportunity to depict emerging work, informally, in a visual format, and share it with a large number of people. Poster sessions typically last about 75–180 min, and are staged in a large auditorium or hotel ballroom. Multiple poster session events may be offered at various times during a conference. Depending upon the size of the conference, the number of posters on display at each session could range from 20 to 80. Unlike the more formal presentations, attendees at poster sessions have the freedom to focus on and engage the presenter in a conversation related to any part of the poster (Miller and Bloustein 2007). Effective poster presentations can give attendees a welcome break from concurrent sessions that are fairly structured and afford additional opportunities to pursue individual interests.

Format

Poster sessions are self-paced. Each presenter is assigned a space where he or she can display their poster. A poster has an orientation different from that of a manuscript; it includes fewer details so that attendees are free to browse and pause whenever something captures their interests (Benis and Benis 2012). When posters

M.R. Jalongo and C. Machado, *Making Effective Presentations at Professional Conferences*, SpringerBriefs in Education,
DOI 10.1007/978-3-319-23174-7_6

are co-presented at least one, if not all, of the presenters are required to oversee the poster for the duration of the session. Attendees move around, pause at posters that interest them and engage the presenter in a conversation. While presenters are not required to prepare an oral presentation, it is always advisable to anticipate questions mentally rehearse responses.

Presenters generally provide a one-page hand-out which includes the contact information of the presenter. Given the popularity of smartphones presenters have begun to add machine-readable QR codes to their poster. This makes it easier for attendees to access their poster digitally and seek additional information following the conference.

How to Propose a Poster

The primary goal of a poster session is to create a compelling visual representation of a project (Benis and Benis 2012). Presenters who are interested in presenting a poster often have to submit a short, succinct abstract. The length of the abstract varies from conference to conference and can range from anywhere between 50–150 words. For details about the format for the abstract presenters need to consult the conference's call for proposals. The type of paper should be reflected in the way the abstract is written. For example, the abstract in Box 6.1 proposes an empirical study. Posters are not necessarily limited to empirical work. Sometimes, they describe community service projects or innovative college curricula, for example.

Box 6.1. Example Abstract for Poster Presentations
Title: Vision Training: Effects on Motor Skills and Visual Ability in Experienced Racquetball Players

This study investigates the effects of vision training on visual ability and motor skills in racquetball players. Fourteen participants were randomly assigned to either a treatment using visual training and traditional racquetball practice, or a control group with practice only. Stereopsis (depth-perception), oculomotor skill (hand-eye coordination), and a sport-specific motor performance (a wall-volley test) were measured before and after 4 weeks of training. The results of these studies will be revealed, and the conclusion that vision training leads to no significant improvements in visual ability or in the transfer to motor performance for racquetball players will be discussed.

Source: http://www.willamette.edu/cla/ssrd/abstract_examples/

In addition to an abstract, some conferences require presenters to include a one to three page description of the project. This generally includes the following:

- Purpose of the Study
- Literature Review/Theoretical Framework
- Methodology
- Results/Findings
- Significance of the Study

Given the word limit deciding exactly what to include and what to leave out is often a challenge for novice writers. Porath has demonstrated in her proposal (see Box 6.2) how the context and theoretical framework can be described succinctly for a data driven paper.

Box 6.2 Excerpt from a Poster Session Proposal: Theoretical Framework Section

Title: Developing Dialogic Pedagogy: Reflecting on Critical Incidents Indicating Teachers' Changing Practices
Authors: Suzanne Porath, Edgewood College and Concordia University
Strand: The Lives of Teachers
Paper Type: Data Driven

Theoretical Framework: This paper draws on Matusov's (2009) theory of dialogic pedagogy which is based on Bakhtin's (1999) theory of dialogism. Classroom designs range on a continuum from more monologic designs where the teacher controls most of the interactions and knowledge acquisition is uncontested to more dialogic designs where student voices are more prevalent and knowledge is constantly tested. In monologic designs, the teacher becomes irrelevant as the curriculum, being predetermined, is considered the determinate of classroom activity and by extension, learning. Within this context, teachers often struggle to author themselves as teachers, not just acquiesce to the authority of the curriculum. On the other hand, in dialogic, authorial teaching (Matusov 2011), many teachers recognize that the standard curriculum needs to be adapted to fit the needs of the teacher, the students, the materials available and the context and it is the interaction of these factors that produce learning, not the curriculum itself. In dialogic pedagogy, education is viewed as a process of meaning-making and knowledge is constantly tested within a community of learners.

Demonstrating that a rigorous approach was used to collect data is also essential. Guo's proposal (see Box 6.3) illustrates how this can be done succinctly.

Box 6.3 Excerpt from a Poster Session Proposal: Methodology Section of a Data Driven Paper

Title: Innovative Research Practice to Engage Preservice Teachers with Religious Diversity

Authors: Yan Guo, University of Calgary

Poster Session: Social Justice and Multiculturalism in Teacher Education

Participants and Data Collection: Two participant groups' experiences were brought together for this study:

Group 1: This paper reports the experiences of 13 Muslim parents who arrived in Calgary after immigrating from India, Pakistan, Bangladesh, Algeria, Somalia, and Suriname. Based on semi-structured interviews of these parents, the larger study presented three types of parent knowledge: cultural knowledge, first language knowledge, and religious knowledge (Author 2012). Then, parent knowledge was shared with a group of pre-service teachers. This paper focused on how pre-service teachers responded to parent religious knowledge.

Group 2: The second participant group in this study consisted of 89 pre-service teachers enrolled in the University of Calgary's Master of Teaching (MT) program, a two-year post-degree bachelor of education program. The pre-service teachers were representative of the nation's teaching force, which is predominantly white and female (Author 2009).

Phase 1: Nine parent leaders were invited to share parent religious knowledge with four groups of pre-service teachers, about 20 students in each group. Each of these dialogues lasted for about 2 h. The discussion groups were held between March, 2009 and March, 2011. The sessions were audio-recorded, and the pre-service teachers' written reflections on these sessions were collected.

Phase 2: The pre-service teachers participated in an on-line forum, in which they were asked to reflect on how, during their field placements, they and their school communities responded to immigrant parents' knowledge on religion. Online prompts included the following:

(a) What is the policy concerning secularism in your school? Do you believe that the school should be secular? Why or why not?
(b) Public education in Canada follows a fundamentalist Christian curriculum and calendar. Do you agree with this statement? Why or why not?
(c) Public schools are obliged to accept religious practices such as permitting Muslim girls to wear headscarves. How does your school accept religious practices? What are your own positions on this issue?
(d) Some Muslim parents in our study requested a prayer space and to exempt their children from certain classes such as dancing and swimming in public schools. How would you respond to these requests in your future teaching?

Phase 3: Focus groups were held with the pre-service teachers to follow up on the questions that had been posed in the online forums. The focus group works well in situations that involve investigating the attitudes and experiences of a homogeneous group of people regarding a specific issue (Krueger and Casey 2000). It allows for meanings to be shared and elaborated upon through group interaction. Focus groups provided a complementary methodology to expand upon the questions posed online. Five focus groups were conducted, and each group included between three and five students. Two students who were unable to attend the focus groups agreed to be interviewed individually.

After presenters are notified that their proposal has been accepted they need to decide on the size and format of the poster, the content to include and general layout, and the composition (visual and textual) of the poster. The size of the poster will depend on the amount of space allocated. This may be listed in the call for proposals and/or the conference website. Presenters are generally allotted a space as small as 3 X 4ft (1X1.3 m) or as large as 3 X 6ft (1.3X2 m) (Benis and Benis 2012). Figure 6.1 presents an example of how the essential elements of a study can be divided into meaningful sections. Headings are included to signify transitions. If the audience is multidisciplinary, presenters should define terms (Roundtree 2010).

Some presenters use a tri-fold poster board (see Fig. 6.1) or software like PowerPoint and/or PosterGenius to reproduce electronic posters on glossy paper (see Figs. 6.2 and 6.3). Others use web2.0 technology like Pinterest and Glogster to create posters that can be projected on a screen with an LCD projector.

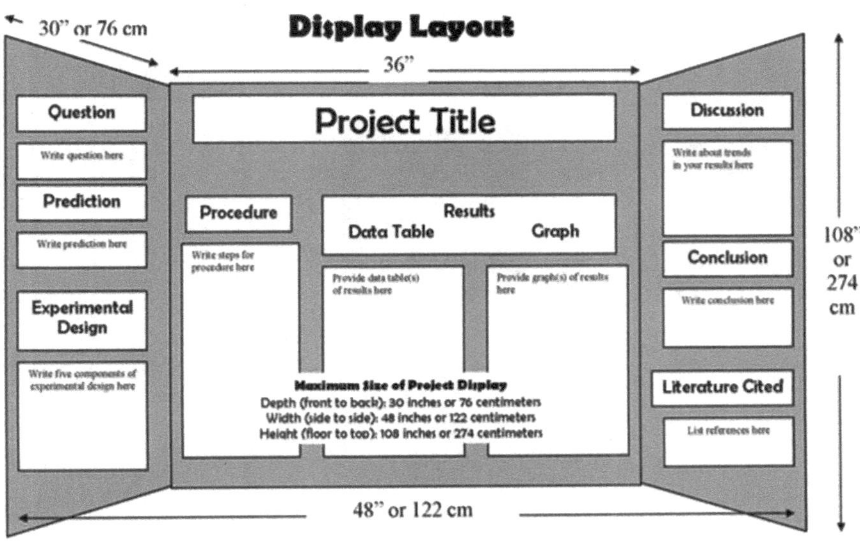

Fig. 6.1 General layout for a poster presentation

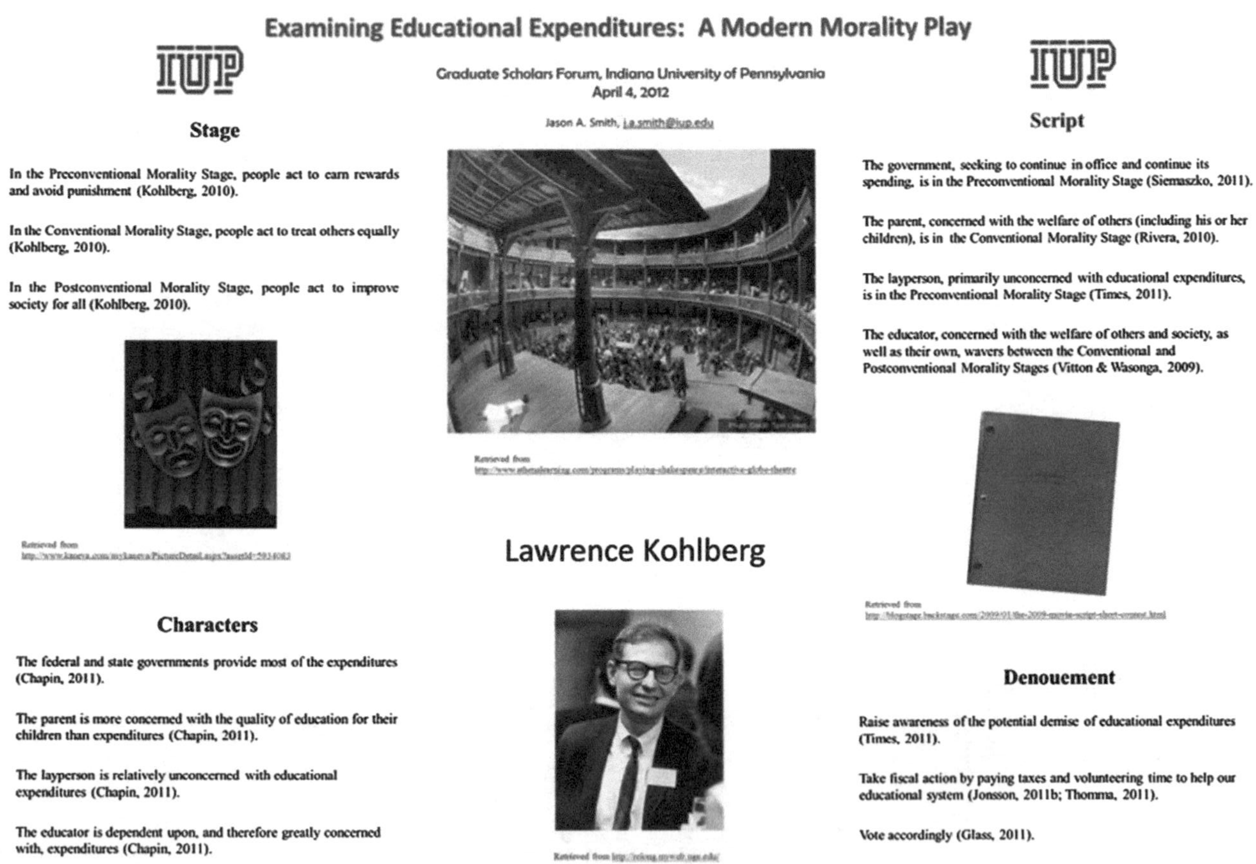

Fig. 6.2 Poster based on a conceptual piece of research

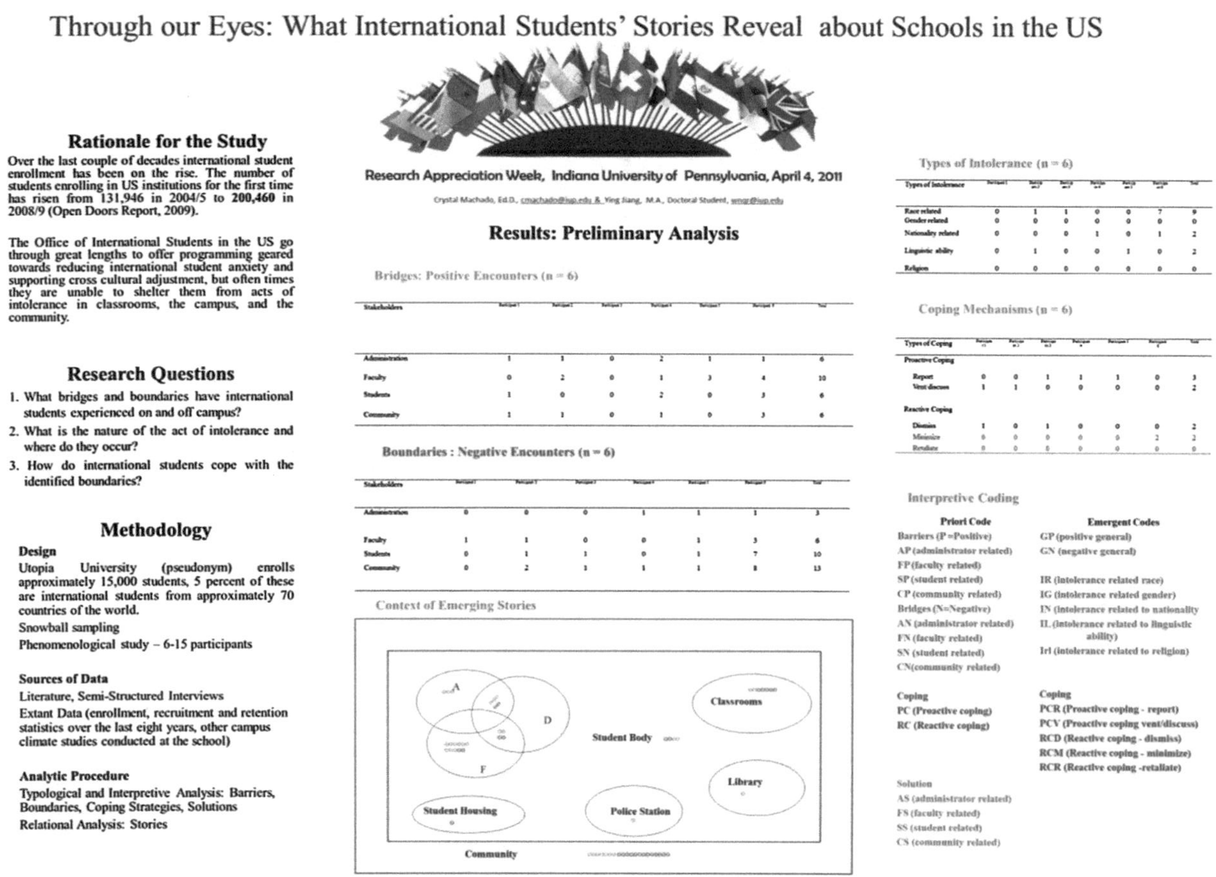

Fig. 6.3 Poster based on a data-driven study

Funding agencies sometimes require scholars to disseminate the results of their work at local forums and conferences. Figure 6.3 highlights how preliminary analysis of a cross-section of the data was presented in poster format. In this case, the presenters engaged attendees in a dialogue about the tabulated data and the list of codes that emerged. They then used the feedback to improve the analytic procedures that were later applied to the entire dataset.

Technology savvy conference attendees, in recent years, have begun to use innovative cloud-based technologies like Prezis, Glogster, and Pinterest to design and present digital posters. These technologies can be used to create, edit, and sync digital posters on the go, on desktops, iPads and Android devices. Presenters can choose a linear or non-linear approach to organize images, videos, animations, and text to describe their research projects. Given that audio and video clips can be embedded into digital posters, they lend themselves to asynchronous sessions. Presenters who opt for these approaches need to verbally rehearse their presentation because the organization of ideas may not be apparent to the attendee. Additionally, with synchronous poster sessions presenters need to check with conference organizers to determine if they will have access to LCD projectors and screens to project the image. If this is not available presenters will need to either take this equipment with them, or use laptops and tablets instead. In the case of the latter they should request a space near a power outlet so that they can keep these devices charged.

Whether the poster is presented on poster board or digitally, presenters need to play close attention to the way content is displayed. Dark backgrounds with light lettering attract attention initially but are tiring to read. A stark contrast between dark letters and a light background makes viewing easier. While the three example posters presented above are all visually appealing Fig. 6.2 is easier on the eye because the presenter has used a larger font size and included more white space. Graphics should be chosen carefully because they can serve as a visual metaphor for text. Additionally, they provide a visual break from reading text. Care should be taken to ensure that the eye catching graphics build on, rather than repeat, textual content.

Presenters should use nonsexist, accountable-talk, not just verbally, but also with text and graphics (consult the APA Manual for guidelines). The Figs. 6.2 and 6.3 illustrate how presenters used both in-text citations and reference lists that meet APA conventions. Presenters should consider using Google's advanced search feature to filter graphics by license, or sites like http://phil.cdc.gov/Phil/home.asp and http://www.nigh.gov/about/hihphotos.htm to locate material in the public domain. The source should be cited under each graphic. Written permission should be obtained for photographs including those of colleagues and/or close friends.

Online Resources for Poster Sessions

Making an Academic Poster Presentation

https://nau.edu/Undergraduate-Research/Poster-Presentation-Tips/

Hosted by Northern Arizona University, this site provides information on the poster's components, content, and design. Brian Thomas from Stanford University provides valuable information about the purpose and benefits of a poster presentation. The site also includes samples posters from a variety of universities and other poster preparation resources.

Creating Effective Poster Presentations

http://www.ncsu.edu/project/posters/

This site maintained by North Carolina State University provides general information about the design of a poster. It also includes links to software options and links to several video critiques of posters.

http://betterposters.blogspot.com/

This blog, which is updated weekly, is a resource for improving posters. Viewers can submit their posters and request a critique. All comments made are moderated. The site also includes links to other information related to conferences and visual presentations in general.

Free PowerPoint Scientific Research Poster Templates

http://www.postersession.com/poster-templates.php

This website provides a library of free PowerPoint templates for poster presentations. In addition to providing access to examples of medical, scientific, and research poster examples the website includes a menu of poster support options.

Checklist for Poster Sessions

Before the Poster Session

- To quickly locate where your poster should be set up, print a copy of the floor plan sent to you by conference organizers. If you did not receive this by email, you may be able to find the floor plan on the conference website or in the conference program.
- Prepare your poster (tri-fold, electronic poster or digital) at least 2 weeks before the conference. If you create a digital poster using Pinterest or any other software save an electronic copy to your laptop so that you can access it with and without internet access.
- Prepare a one-page handout. This could be a copy of your poster, or a bulleted list of information listed on your poster. In addition to the content, the title of the poster, the date, your contact information and a QR code on the first slide. The QR code will make it possible for attendees to access your material digitally. Take at least 10–15 handouts with you.

- Save an electronic copy of your poster and handouts on a flash drive and email a copy to yourself. Additionally, save your presentation material and handouts on a flash drive and/or in the cloud if you use Google Drive or Dropbox so you can access your material if your laptop fails to function.
- Take business cards to share with attendees who might like to contact you later.
- On the day of the session use the session number or title of the poster session and the floor plan provided to identify the location of your poster.
- Be prepared to set up your poster at least 30 min before the session is scheduled to begin.

During the Poster Session

- Place your one-page handouts near the poster so that they attendees can access them readily.
- Position yourself to the side of the poster rather than in front of it so attendees can view your poster and decide if they wish to engage you in conversation. Do not be discouraged if people walk by; this is the nature of a poster session.
- Avoid getting so involved in conversations with co-authors or the presenters near you that viewers hesitate to interrupt the conversation (Benis and Benis 2012).
- Provide the attendees who approach your poster with an opportunity to read your poster. Offer to tell them about your poster if they display, by their body language, a desire to engage in conversation. Inquire about the work they have done in this area.
- Attempt to answer all questions. If you are unable to answer certain questions offer to do so by email.
- Listen attentively to their recommendations and take notes. Ask for their contact information, if appropriate, so that you can continue the conversation, either by phone or email.

After the Poster Session

- Mingle with other poster presenters as they prepare to leave. Give them your business card, if requested.
- Keep a record of all questions and comments from attendees for future reference.
- Send an email to attendees who contributed ideas or information that you intend to use to refine your manuscript.

References

Beins, B. C. & Beins, A. M. (2012). *Effective writing in psychology: Papers, posters, and presentations* (2nd ed.). New York, NY: John Wiley.

Miller, J. E., & Bloustein, E. J. (2007). Preparing and presenting effective research posters. *Health Services Research, 42*(1), 311–328.

Roundtree, A. (2010). http://www.uhd.edu/academic/colleges/sciences/scholars/files/workshop-poster.pdf.

Chapter 7
Paper Sessions

Most paper sessions at conferences feature the authors of three to five different papers that have been grouped thematically. Attendees have an opportunity to engage in discussion with the presenters and discussant during the latter part of the session.

Scope

Paper sessions, often perceived to be more prestigious that roundtable or poster sessions, provide a group of author/researchers with an opportunity to share abbreviated versions of their work with interested members of the organization. Because these sessions are organized by themes and offered concurrently, presenters can expect anywhere between 8–30 attendees. Topics that are very timely are scheduled in larger rooms and could be attended by 30–60. On average, a paper session lasts approximately an hour with each presenter allocated just 8–20 minutes. Presenters can use the feedback received from other authors, the chair and/or discussant of the session, and participants to improve the manuscript prior to submitting it for publication.

Format

At many conferences, paper sessions take place in rooms with a theatre style (chairs only) configuration, and a head table for five to eight presenters next to the podium. Seated at the head table are the chair, the authors of three to five papers, and the discussant. The chair, who plays a leadership role, welcomes presenters and the discussant at least 10 min before the session begins and helps them establish a reasonable comfort level with the room arrangement, technology, time limitations,

M.R. Jalongo and C. Machado, *Making Effective Presentations at Professional Conferences*, SpringerBriefs in Education,
DOI 10.1007/978-3-319-23174-7_7

and sequence of presentation. The chair calls the session to order at the scheduled time, introduces the session and the presenters, manages time, and ensures that the session schedule is followed. If a presenter has to cancel at the last minute, the chair maintains continuity and adjusts the time allocated to each paper accordingly.

Each presenter, on average, is allocated 8–15 min, depending upon the number of papers in the session, to present the paper orally to a room that could include anywhere between 5–60 attendees. Presenters are given approximately five minutes to respond to questions, either immediately after their presentation, or at the end, after all the papers have been delivered. When papers are presented by multiple authors they need to figure out who will be responsible for speaking. They may decide that one presenter will present the paper while others respond to questions.

Paper sessions typically conclude with the discussant's remarks and/or critique. Discussants are selected for their expertise in the content area. Well before the conference, discussants are given access to all papers so they can do a close reading of each paper and prepare their remarks. Knowing this helps to explain why it is so important to submit papers on time—otherwise, it will be an imposition on the discussant. Their remarks typically include constructive criticism about the scope of the study, research design, findings, and implications. They often highlight the interrelationship among the papers represented and summarize the contributions of the work to the broader stream of literature. If time permits, they highlight controversial issues and stimulate a dialogue among those in attendance. If a discussant has not been appointed, the chair may carry out this role.

How to Propose a Paper

The length of a paper submitted for a paper session depends to a large extent on the popularity and selectivity of the conference. Some conferences base acceptance on their review of abstracts. Others provide the presenters with an option to submit for a brief (1–3 pages) or full paper session (5–6 pages) at the proposing stage. Presenters of full-papers are allocated slightly more time to present. Some conferences require presenters to submit a more developed paper of approximately 15–20 pages a few weeks before the conference. Presenters who are working on a new idea or have not presented at a conference for a while should opt for one that requires an abstract rather than a developed paper so they can work at their own pace.

Presenters with a more complete project should consider proposing a brief or full paper. The feedback provided, whether the proposal is selected on not, will facilitate manuscript preparation. When given the option, presenters should select the "brief/full" paper option only if they have the time to devote to manuscript preparation. If required, presenters should submit a copy of their paper to the discussant before the conference date. This provides the discussant with enough time to read and reflect on the paper, thus enhancing the quality of the feedback he or she can provide immediately after formal presentation of the paper. It will also save presenters the embarrassment of being confronted by an annoyed discussant who starts his remarks by announcing, as some have done, that the paper arrived too late to formulate any substantive thoughts about it (Kerber 2008).

The guidelines for data-driven and methods papers are typically very clear. These papers generally include the following sections:

- Introduction
- Review of Literature
- Methodology
- Analysis/Results/Key findings
- Discussion/Implication
- Conclusions/Recommendations

The expectation that the proposal be limited to three pages for a brief paper, or six pages for a full paper, can be challenging for beginning scholars. Given that 10 or 15-minute time limits are common, focus on a few, key talking points. Avoid inundating the reader (and audience, at a later stage) with information that has the potential to bore or confuse them (Platow 2002). Successful proposals include essential information and presenters assume that those who want considerably more detail will contact them after the presentation. Box 7.1 presents an example of how the methodology and results can be discussed succinctly.

Box 7.1. Except from a Paper Proposal: Research Methodology and Data Section

Title: Advocacy for English Language Learners: The Role of English-as-a-Second Language Teacher

Authors: Heather A. Linville, University of Wisconsin, LaCrosse

Paper Session: Supporting Immigrant Learners Though Practice and Advocacy

Research Methodology and Data: To address the research questions, data were collected from a large scale 27 item survey of ESOL teachers in four school districts within one Mid Atlantic state (n = 482). Following Borg's (2006) elements of teacher cognition, survey items collected participant demographic data on the following control variables: age, gender, race, U.S. born or not, number of languages spoken, experience traveling or living abroad, where and when they completed ESOL certification, number of years of teaching experience, grades taught, and knowledge of the TESOL/NCATE standards. Contextual information was also collected; the number of other ESOL teachers at the school, SES of school where teaching, and level of perceived support of advocacy for ELLs by others in schools (Table 1)

Participants' average age was 45 and they had an average of 10 years of ESOL teaching experience. The population was more likely to teach elementary school than middle or high school. Almost 2 % of the population was not certified while 19 % had ESOL certification as an add on to another certification. A high percentage of the population (79 %) received their certification after 2000 (the year the Standards were implemented), and their knowledge of the Standards fell in the "minimal" to "some" range for the majority of participants.

Survey items designed to answer the research questions of this study were created from the Standards, the Teacher Social Justice Awareness Scale (Barazanji 2012), and author created items, previously piloted, on critical language awareness. Each survey statement was assessed on a 6 point (1 = strongly disagree to 6 = strongly agree) Likert type scale. Exploratory factor analysis was utilized to determine which survey items measured similar constructs. Four constructs were identified and scales were created to reflect these: Advocacy Acts Scale, Social Justice Awareness Scale, Standard English Scale, and Critical Language Awareness Scale. Additional survey items were created from the hypothesized teacher cognition (Borg 2006) factors related to advocacy beliefs.

Results: An overwhelming 70 % of participants believe that advocacy is a part of their professional responsibilities as an ESOL teacher. An additional 24 % agree and 5 % somewhat agree. In fact, only1 % of the respondents indicated that they do not believe that advocacy is a part of their ESOL teaching role. Descriptive results further indicate that the participants have a very high level of social justice awareness and understand to a high degree the role that discrimination plays in language learning and teaching. The Advocacy Acts Scale has a mean score of 4.03, indicating that the participants on average self report that they carry out the advocacy acts included in that scale (see Appendix, Table 2).

Further exploration of the Advocacy Acts Scale reveals that participants self-report the least acts of social/political advocacy (following Lewis et al. 2003). Taking a leadership role in the community with respect to issues affecting ELLs and lobbying public officials to challenge negative policies related to ELLs and their families received the lowest levels of agreement (55 and 26 % respectively). Teacher variables positively associated with their responses on the Advocacy Acts Scale include number of years teaching, number of languages spoken, level of perceived support for advocacy in the school, and the level of perceived emphasis on advocacy in the ESOL certification program.

The excerpt from DeZeeuw, Baverkemper and Walker's proposal in Box 7.2 illustrates how the procedures to collect data and enhance trustworthiness can be described.

Box 7.2. Except from a Paper Proposal: Data Sources and Analysis
Title: An Innovative Framework for Math and Science Teacher Professional Development: The UTeach Observation Protocol as a Lens for Feedback and Reflection.
Authors: Audrey DeZeeuw, Paige Baverkemper, and Mary H. Walker; The University of Texas, Austin

Paper Session: Professional Learning in STEM Areas
Data Sources: The UTOP pilot professional development process used many data sources. The first set of data gathered was of the teacher's classroom practice using the UTOP instrument. Content experts observed participant classrooms and conducted over 100 classroom observations. This observational data was then aggregated according to campus and disaggregated according to individuals. Teachers also attended two trainings conducted by UTOP experts and completed surveys via Qualtrics about their experience and suggestions for the trainings. Once teachers were trained on the instrument they received their individual and campus scores during confidential data sharing sessions with the UTOP expert that observed their classroom. After participants were trained and received feedback they chose domains of the instrument they wanted to focus on and scheduled observations of a peer. Participants conducted two peer observations, one with a researcher for final calibration purposes and a final observation on their own.

Classroom observations, data reveal sessions, teacher peer observations, as well as open-ended surveys were conducted with all the participants between September 2011 and May 2013. Interviews and surveys generated data regarding participants' perspectives on UTOP trainings, individual feedback sessions and the peer observation process. The interviews and surveys were designed purposefully to provide triangulation and saturation of data results to increase internal and external validity.

Data Analysis: All interviews and data reveal reflections were transcribed and identifying information removed or masked. Open ended survey responses were de-identified but not transcribed as they were imported from the Qualtrics software. Three researchers coded the interviews using open-coding techniques reflecting emergent categories (Glaser and Strauss 1967). As we engaged with the coding we discussed emergent memos, shared these across researchers, and continued exploring the patterns until we were able to answer our research questions.

UTOP observation data, both individual and campus, were in two graphs, one campus and one individual. Both graphs were arranged in decreasing order of average indicator score. Each color on the indicator bars represents a different score, ranging from 1 to 5. The proportion for each color on the bar represents the percentage of observations with the corresponding score (see Fig. 1). Using the same scale and display for campus and individual data was a user-friendly way for participants to identify similarities and differences between their individual performance and their campus.

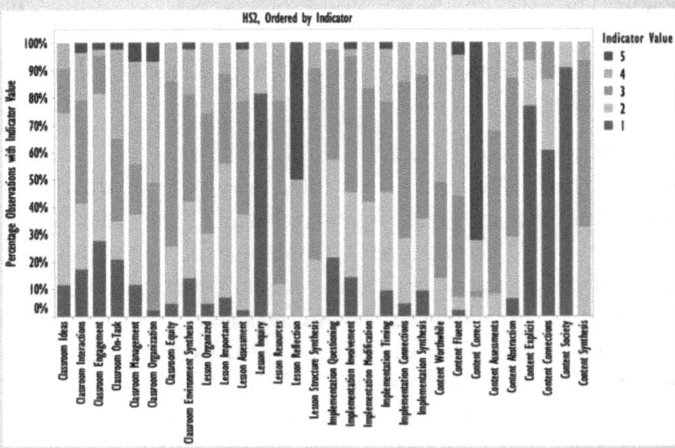

Fig. 1 Example UTOP score profile

Presenters need to acknowledge limitations of the study (see Box 7.3). The strength of a proposal can be enhanced further by describing the steps taken to minimize research bias and other limitations. To learn more about research bias that has the potential to compromise data quality, visit https://explorable.com/research-bias.

Box 7.3. Excerpt from a Paper Proposal: Limitations of the Study
Title: Technology Integration in K-12 Classrooms: The Impact of Graduate Coursework on Teachers' Knowledge and Practice
Authors: Crystal Machado and DeAnna Laverick, Indiana University of Pennsylvania
Paper Session: Technology, Pedagogy and Content Knowledge (TPACK)

Limitations: The limitations of this study relate to its context and subjectivity. The learning environment reflected a unique setting that may be difficult to replicate in other situations. The small sample may not be representative of all K-12 teachers and generalized implications should be taken with caution. As a Scholarship of Teaching and Learning (SoTL) project, the views of the researchers, who were also the course instructors and participant observers, could have been inevitably influenced by preconceived ideas and available resources.

Finally, presenters need to convince the reader that their work adds to the existing body of knowledge as Sheth and Braaten have done in the excerpt provided in Box 7.4.

Box 7.4. Except from a Paper Proposal: Significance of the Study Section
Title: Doing Better: Illuminating Teachers' Multiple Pathways to Equitable Science Pedagogy (ESP)
Authors: Manali I. Sheth, Iowa State University and Melissa Lee Braaten, University of Wisconsin-Madison
Paper Session: Critical Issues in Science Teaching and Learning

Significance of the Study: This study contributes to Science and multicultural education research in several ways. First, through rich descriptions and cross-case analyses of teachers' classroom enactments and visions, we provide practice-based examples of ESP to support teachers and teacher educators in working towards equitable science pedagogies. Additionally, this study presents a holistic framework that can support the development of resources for supporting pre- and in-service teachers in becoming more equitable science teachers. By working at the intersection of educational theory, teacher theories, and teachers' pedagogies, this framework illuminates the kinds of decision making involved in equitable science teaching and the various problems of practice that arise. Findings can provoke teachers and teacher educators to identify challenges and affordances of existing visions/enactments and imagine other pathways.

The guidelines for papers of a theoretical nature, consciousness-raising, perspective, agenda setting, review and position papers are not always detailed in a call for proposals. As a first step towards writing a strong proposal presenters should create an outline to organize their thoughts. Outlines serve many purposes. Murray (2013) maintains that outlines facilitate idea generation, provide a structure, link ideas clarify the contributions, create coherence, eliminate extraneous information, provide direction, and contextualize the work. Becker (2014) recommends limiting an outline to six points, jotted down in 1 min, because it forces you to look at the "bigger picture" and include only that which is important. The outline presented in Box 7.5 began with idea generation. The structure became coherent, over a period of time, as the co-authors linked and eliminated ideas.

Prior to submission presenters are advised to evaluate the quality of their proposal either themselves, or with the help of a peer. This can be done with the help of the criteria outlined in Box 7.6.

Box 7.5. Example Outline for a Paper Session Title: Using Twitter to Heighten Student Engagement, Critical Thinking and Reflective Practice Within and Beyond the Classroom
Authors: Crystal Machado and Ying Jiang, Indiana University of Pennsylvania
Paper Session: Teaching with Technology in Higher Education

Introduction
Influence of Social Media across Disciplines
Teaching with Twitter
The Use of Twitter in the K-12 Classroom
The Use of Twitter in the Higher Education Classroom
Can Twitter Be Used to Promote Critical Thinking and Reflective Practice in Educational Professionals?
One Professor of Education, Five Courses, Many Tweets, Much Learning
An Invitation to Faculty to Engage in Pedagogical Exploration with Twitter

Box 7.6. Proposal Evaluation Criteria

1. The paper is short, preferably five pages long.
2. The purpose of the paper is reflected in the title, the abstract, and the introduction.
3. The introduction begins generally, is followed with a description of the context in a line or two, makes an assertion that captivates the audience, and follows with statements supported with authoritative evidence. Finally, it restates the thesis (Jalongo 2013).
4. The body of the paper includes headings that show transition from one section to the next.
5. The body of the proposal includes tables which reduce the word count of the main body of the manuscript (Pavlovich-Danis 2014). Each has a clearly defined title, column headings, data fields, and a foot note, that helps the reader to understand the table and the data it represents.
6. The recommendations in the conclusion relate closely to the stated purpose, and are supported by data that were presented in the analysis section.
7. The proposal meets the formatting and style conventions outlined in the call for paper. While major conferences in the field of education require presenters to meet APA conventions, conference organizers do reserve the right to modify this expectation. For example, the Society for Information Technology and Teacher Education (SITE) conference requires attendees to use their template.

Online Resources for Paper Sessions

Some Tips for Preparing a Research Presentation
http://www.cs.swarthmore.edu/~newhall/presentation.html
This site provides information about how a presentation should be organized, how slides should be designed, and how presenters should prepare and practice their talk. It also includes links to other oral presentation advice.

How to Convert your Paper into a Presentation
http://twp.duke.edu/uploads/media_items/paper-to-talk.original.pdf
Prepared by the Thomson Writing Program at Duke University, this document provides general tips that will benefit novice presenters. It discusses conference culture and includes links to other resources.

Designing PowerPoint Slides for a Scientific Presentation
https://www.youtube.com/watch?v=1fs_jqXGs8s
The presenter in this You-tube clip describes the importance of presenting each slide as a message unit. He describes how information should be displayed on slides with word tables, data tables, graphs, builds etc. Finally he demonstrates with examples how this can be done effectively.

13 Best Practice Tips for Effective Presentation Handouts
http://www.speakingaboutpresenting.com/delivery/presentation-handouts/
Olivia Mitchell describes how handouts, which are a concrete manifestation of a presentation, can be designed more effectively.

Checklist for Paper Sessions

Before the Paper Session

- Print a copy of the session as described in the conference program and/or the conference website. This will make it possible for you to identify and address the chair and other presenters by name when when you introduce yourself.
- Prepare presentation materials a week ahead of time. This could include the paper itself, a one-page handout that summarizes the paper, a document that includes charts and tables that you hope to discuss with particpants, and/or a data collection instrument that you wish to share with attendees. In addition to the content include a cover page with the title of the paper, the date, your contact information and a QR code on the first slide. The QR code will make it possible for attendees to access your material digitally and contact you later if they wish to reuse the material. Take at least 15 handouts with you.
- Review the conference websites and call for proposal to determine if the room will be equipped with a laptop and/or LCD projector. If you are not able to

locate this information take your laptop with you. The battery should be charged because you may not be close enough to a power outlet.

- If you plan to use digital techology like a PowerPoint, Prezi, or a Pinterest board to support delivery of content save a copy on your laptop so you can present your work in a timely fashion, whether you have acces to the internet or not
- Save your presentation material and handouts on a flash drive and/or in the cloud if you use Google Drive or Dropbox so you can access your material if your laptop fails to function.
- Take business cards to share with attendees who might like to contact you later.
- Use the session number and title of the paper to identify the room where you will present prior to the session. If possible, visit the room in advance to make sure that the set up is satisfactory.

During the Paper Session

- Reach the room at least 15 min before your session is scheduled to begin. Introduce yourself to the chair, and other presenters, if they are present. If not, you can start setting up the equipment. If a laptop has been provided, you can transfer your presentation to the desktop of the laptop and encourage other presenters to do the same. This facilitates a smoother transition from one presentation to the next. If a laptop is not provided, you can offer to use your laptop.
- Listen attentively to the chair's instructions about the protocol that will be followed. Some conferences require chairs to follow a pre-determined protocol, while others give chairs the freedom to decide how the session will be managed.
- Listen attentively to other presenters and take notes so you can contribute meaningfully when the discussion ensues.
- Distribute your one-page handout to everyone who is seated at the table just before you begin your presentation. Direct participants' attention to interesting trends and patterns in the data. Indicate the nature of the feedback you would like to receive and make the contributions and limitations of the work clear.
- Introduce yourself, and then proceed with the presentation. Do not read the content included in your presentation material and/or handouts. Instead, use a conversational tone to describe your study and summarize your results.
- Manage your presentation time appropriately either with the assistance of the chair or with a cell phone application that keeps time.
- Keep a record of all questions and comments from the audience members for future reference.

After the Paper Session

- Approach attendees who showed a special interest in your topic and inquire about the work they have done in this area.
- Interact with other presenters, the chair, and attendees as they prepare to leave. Offer your business card to those who are receptive.
- Thank the session chair personally at the end of the session, or later by email.

- Keep a record of all questions and comments from attendees for future reference.
- Follow up with individuals who hold promise as co-presenters or co-authors.

Appendix

Table 1 Response rate by school district with ELL population information

District	Description	ELL population (%)	Free/Reduced lunch (%)	Response rate (%)
1	Urban	4	84	38
2	Suburban	4	45	46
3	Suburban	12	60	46
4	Suburban	13	32	44
				Total N = 482

Table 2 Descriptive and reliability information for survey scales

Scale	Mean	Standard deviation	Cronbach's alpha
Advocacy acts	4.03	0.757	0.848
Social justice awareness	5.45	0.576	0.807
Standard english	2.93	1.13	0.643
Language discrimination	4.99	0.788	0.807

References

Becker, L. (2014). *Presenting your research: Conferences, symposiums, poster presentations and beyond.* Los Angeles, CA: Sage.

Jalongo, M. R. (2013). Getting on the conference program and writing a practical article: Templates for success. *Early Childhood Education Journal, 41*, 13–23.

Kerber, L. (2008). Conference rules: Everything you need to know about presenting a scholarly paper in public. Retrieved June 8, 2015 from http://www.historians.org/publications-and-directories/perspectives-on-history/may-2008/conference-rules-everything-you-need-to-know-about-presenting-a-scholarly-paper-in-public.

Murray, R. (2013). *Writing for academic journals*. Boston, MA: Pearson.

Pavlovich-Danis, S. J. (2014). All about tables, figures, graphs, illustrations, and photos. In C. Saver (Ed.), *Anatomy of writing for publication for nurses* (pp. 113–134). Indianapolis, IN: Sigma Theta Tau International.

Platow, M. (2002). *Giving professional presentations in the behavioral sciences and related fields.* New York, NY: Psychology Press.

Chapter 8
Symposia/Panel Discussions

Symposia and panel discussions are similar in many ways. They both consist of a small group of presenters who share differing ideas related to a common theme, issue, or question, and then discuss them with the audience. The symposium often consists of scholarly research conducted independently by the different presenters while, a panel discussion frequently is a forum for research or expertise that panelists have gained over a period of time.

Scope

Conferences offer proportionately fewer symposia/panel sessions than paper sessions. These sessions are perceived to be as prestigious as paper presentations. They generally include the authors of three to five papers that present differing viewpoints, a chair, and discussant. When viewpoints are shared, panelists may choose to focus on different aspects. Presenters of both symposia and/or panels share the results of individual projects with attendees. Each presenter's paper or oral delivery, contributes to the examination of a specific research issue, problem or topic; thus providing attendees with a range of contrasting points of view, interpretations, and solutions related to an issue, problem, or topic. Because these sessions are organized by themes and offered concurrently presenters can expect anywhere between 8–30 attendees. Topics that are very timely are scheduled in larger rooms and could be attended by 30–60 attendees. A symposium/panel discussion is the best format when the goal is to examine a topic, trend, issue, or controversy and to contribute to the professional dialogue through interaction among experts.

Format

Unlike other concurrent sessions, which are organized by conference organizers or section chairs, symposia/panels are organized by the presenters. They assume responsibility for proposing a topic that aligns with the theme of the conference,

M.R. Jalongo and C. Machado, *Making Effective Presentations at Professional Conferences*, SpringerBriefs in Education,
DOI 10.1007/978-3-319-23174-7_8

identifying presenters, describing the format to be used during the session, and putting the proposal together. Additionally, the proposers identify a chairperson for the panel. Session organizers, who include work from a single unit, may be required to include a discussant that is external to the project, group, or team. This makes for a richer discussion and provides panelists with constructive critique and commentary which can be used to delve further into the concept and refine a manuscript.

Symposia/panel discussions are generally 90 min long. Conferences sometimes provide session organizers with the option to request a session that lasts 120 min. These longer sessions may be limited in number. Additionally, they are often scheduled at the beginning or end of the day. Symposia/panel discussions can take on many different forms. Some employ a panel discussion or a town meeting format that centers on an issue or problem. Others are more interactive in nature and include small group interaction, discussion among presenters and discussant, or a discussion among all those present. Either way, presenters should take no more than 60 % of the total time to present well-reasoned arguments about pertinent topics from a variety of viewpoints. Following the individual paper presentations the discussant, chair, and attendees engage in dialogue about the issues presented.

Sessions take place in rooms with a theatre style (chairs only) configuration, and a head table for 4–8 presenters next to the podium. Seated at the head table is the session organizer who also serves as the chair, the authors of the papers, and the discussant, when included. The chair plays a leadership role, welcomes presenters and the discussant at least ten minutes before the session begins and helps them establish a reasonable comfort level with the room arrangement, technology, and sequence of presentation and time limitations. The chair then calls the session to order at the scheduled time, describes the session structure, and introduces the presenters. The chair manages time and ensures that the session schedule is followed. If presenters cancel at the last minute the chair adjusts the schedule accordingly.

How to Propose a Symposium/Panel Discussion

Symposia/panel discussions are generally chosen based on the prominence of the presenters in the field, timeliness of the topic, originality of the proposal, and the potential to engage attendees in an informative and controversial discussion. Proposals generally include the following elements:

- A title
- A brief 120–150 words abstract that is made publically available online and in print
- A 500 word session summary that includes (a) the session's objectives (b) an overview of the presentation and (c) the significance of the presentation
- A 500 word summary and list of references for each paper included in the symposium.

The primary objective is to facilitate an exchange of differing viewpoints. For example, if the discussion is about the appropriateness of electronic portfolios as a learning/assessment tool, the symposium could include papers in support of, and in opposition to this form of learning and assessment. Conversely, a group of like-minded presenters from different institutions where electronic portfolios are in wide use might present on particular aspects (e.g., needs assessment, planning, implementation, and evaluation). A richer discussion ensues when the panel is varied, as in Box 8.1. The papers included in this symposium gave researchers in teacher education, policy makers and practitioners access to research studies, analytic techniques, and theoretical frameworks that put the spotlight on Black males' cultural strengths.

In special circumstances, a symposium/panel may include a number of presenters from the same institution or geographic region, as is the case with Kara Viesca and her colleagues' proposal (see Box 8.2). As evident from the titles of papers, the abstract, and the scholarly significance, this symposium presents the work of content faculty, language acquisition specialists, and instructional technology experts who collaboratively designed and implemented online professional development for teachers to improve their practices working with multilingual learners. Additionally, this proposal showcases diversity in terms of research methodologies.

Box 8.1 Excerpt from a Symposium: Overview of the Presentation and Papers

Symposium Title: Erasing the Deficits: Contemporary Perspectives on successfully Educating Black Males for High Academic Achievement

Papers and Authors:

1. Reframing Resilience: Amalgamating Postcolonial and Border Theory to Appreciate Black Bermudian Male Success; Ty-Ron M. O. Douglas, University of Missouri-Columbia;
2. I am trying to get my A": Black Male Achievers Talk about Race, School and Achievement; Quaylan Allen, Chapman University
3. "Leaving Bread Crumbs Along the Way": Developing Mentor Relationships that Facilitate School Success for African-American Male Students; Jonathan Andrew Carroll, University of California, Los Angeles

Chair: Chezare A. Warren, Michigan State University
Discussant: Tyrone C. Howard, University of California—Los Angeles
Overview of the Presentation: The chair will give opening remarks, which will include an overview of key findings from the New York City Black and Latino Male Achievement Study (NYCBLMA). The NYCBLMA examined the student-level, institutional, familial, and community factors influencing the high academic achievement of Black and Latino males who attend (ed) one of forty historically low-performing public neighborhood high schools in New York City. The study includes in-depth interviews with 411 participants. Following his remarks, the chair will introduce each panelist and

the order their papers are to be presented. Next, the discussant will provide a critical review of each paper and offer recommendations. The discussant will then facilitate an interactive dialogue between symposium attendees and panelists. Finally, the chair will offer brief closing remarks and adjourn the session.

Box 8.2 Excerpt from a Symposium: Abstract and Scholarly Significance Symposium Title: Improving the Education of Multilingual Learners and their Teachers through Interdisciplinary Collaborations and Online Professional Development

Papers and Authors

1. Collaborative Interdisciplinary Design for Pedagogical Language Knowledge, Kara Mitchell Viesca and Honorine D. Nocon, University of Colorado;
2. Learning to Teach Fractions to Multilingual Learners: The Intersection of Online Learning and Professional Development, Jacqueline Leonard, University of Wyoming and Nicole Michelle Joseph, University of Denver;
3. Developing Linguistic Responsiveness in Science Teachers of Multilingual Learners, Geeta K. Verma, Helen Douglass and Boni Hamilton, University of Colorado;
4. Lessons Learned: Reframing Teachers' Perceptions of Bilingual Students, Sheila M. Shannon, Elizabeth Mahon, and Nancy Commins, University of Colorado

Chair: Cindy Gutierrez, University of Colorado, Denver
Discussant: Tamara F. Lucas, Montclair State University

Abstract: Multilingual learners, commonly referred to as English language learners (ELLs), are the fastest growing student subgroup in the United States and have been for some time (Goldenberg and Coleman 2010). Supporting the academic and linguistic development of multilingual learners is no longer only the work of English as a Second Language specialists and bilingual educators. Rather, every classroom teacher needs to have the skills, dispositions, and knowledge to be culturally and linguistically responsive (Lucas et al. 2008; Villegas and Lucas 2002). This session presents empirical research on the work of content faculty, language acquisition specialists, and instructional technology experts who collaboratively designed and implemented online professional development for teachers to improve their practices working with multilingual learners.

Scholarly Significance: There is still a great deal that we need to learn about educating teachers of multilingual learners (Lucas 2011), particularly through innovative online technologies and approaches. Further, there is still a great deal we need to learn about how to meaningfully intersect content and language instruction in K-12 classrooms to provide a high-quality education for multilingual learners. Therefore, this collection of research studies will contribute substantially to our understandings about improving educator development through interdisciplinary approaches in an innovative online professional learning setting.

Incluing discussants from a different institutions (see Box 8.1 and 8.2), increases the opportunity to get valuable feedback.

In addition to an overall symposium summary session organizers include a 500 word summary written by the authors of each paper. As apparent from the excerpt presented in Box 8.3 authors have to succinctly convey the objectives of the study, theoretical perspective, modes of inquiry, data sources, results, significance, and references. Given the word limit data tables that are referenced in the summary are included after the reference list rather than part of the summary.

Box 8.3 Excerpt from a Symposium: Summary of a Paper Included Symposium Paper #2:
Title: Aligning the Early Math Professional Development with Teachers' Zone of Proximal Development

Authors: Jie-Qi Chen, Erikson Institute Jennifer McCray, Erikson Institute Bilge Cerezci, Erikson Institute
Objectives: This presentation describes an Investing in Innovation (i3) fund professional development (PD) project designed to improve the mathematical competence of teachers from prekindergarten through grade 3. A highlight of the PD is its design and implementation based on clearly identified needs of the teachers.
Perspectives: Numerous studies indicate that high quality early mathematics education builds a strong foundation for future mathematics learning and school success (Duncan et al. 2007; Jordan et al. 2009). Despite its importance, many early childhood teachers are not adequately prepared to provide engaging and rigorous mathematics education (NAEYC and NCTM 2002/2010). Of critical importance to increasing teachers' proficiency in early math teaching is their continued learning through effective PD (NRC 2009). Among many contributing factors to effective PD, meeting the specific needs of teachers is highly recommended but seldom done successfully (Darling-Hammond et al. 2009).

Modes of Inquiry: In our work with approximately 120 PreK-Grade 3 teachers in eight Chicago public schools, we used the High-Impact Strategies

Table 1 Domains and dimensions of high-impact strategies in early math

Domains—the degree to which observed teacher practice demonstrates	Dimensions—the degree to which observed teacher practice emphasizes
1. A deep knowledge of foundational mathematics concepts—the what domain	1. Learning objectives
	2. Mathematical representations
	3. Concept development
2. An understanding of children's typical development and individual variations in math learning—the who domain	4. Attention to developmental trajectories
	5. Response to individual students' needs
	6. Developmentally appropriate learning formats
3. The effective use of mathematics teaching strategies—the how domain	7. Planning
	8. Student engagement
	9. Establishment of math learning community

for Early Mathematics (HIS-EM) to gauge the quality of mathematics teaching in the classroom and plan the intervention accordingly. The HIS-EM, a validated teacher observation tool, consists of nine dimensions, each scored on a 7-point scale (see Table 1). The observation was conducted at baseline, and at the end of each school year for four years. Results influenced programmatic decisions to increase PD effectiveness.

Data Sources: Baseline observations were gathered for 108 intervention and 102 comparison teachers. No significant differences between groups occurred on any HI-SEM dimensions. For the intervention group, means fall in the middle range from 3.75 to 4.13. The lowest mean among the nine dimensions is concept development (M = 3.75), followed by use of developmentally appropriate learning formats (M = 3.81), response to individual students' needs (M = 3.89), and planning (M = 3.93) (see Table 2).

Following interpretation of the baseline data, the project developed a range of strategies. For example, greater emphasis was placed on the use of *Big Ideas* in early math meant to strengthen teachers' conceptual understanding of foundational mathematics. *Research Lessons* were introduced to draw teachers' attention to developmentally appropriate learning experiences and individual learners. *Cognitive Coaching* was increased to ensure that teachers engaged in the planning process.

Results: As shown in Table 3, the intervention teachers improved in all nine HI-SEM dimensions from T1 to T2. A t-test showed marginally significant differences between the two observations, and a strong trend in favor of teachers' performance in T2, $t(95) = 1.93$, $p = 0.056$, T1(M = 35.8, SD = 1.60), T2(M = 38.5, SD = 1.28). Further, the intervention teachers performed significantly better than the comparison group at T2, $t(189) = 4.61$, $p < 0.05$, Intervention (M = 38.5, SD = 1.28, Comparison (M = 31.8,

Table 2 Descriptive statistics of quality mathematics practice of intervention teachers

Domains and dimensions	N	Range	M	SD
What				
Learning objectives	108	1–7	4.06	1.52
Mathematical representations	108	2–7	4.13	1.47
Concept development	108	1–7	3.75	1.58
Who				
Attention to developmental trajectories	108	1–7	4.03	1.56
Response to individual students' needs	108	1–7	3.89	1.62
Developmentally appropriate learning formats	108	1–7	3.81	1.60
How				
Planning	108	1–7	3.93	1.63
Student engagement	108	1–7	4.11	1.71
Establishment of math learning community	108	1–7	4.10	1.75

SD = 1.54). Year 2 data is being analyzed and more positive changes are anticipated.

Significance: The present work tested the power of designing PD to meet the specific needs of teachers. This approach recognizes and values teachers' experience while providing support in response to their needs. It turns PD into a learning opportunity for its designers and increases its chances of producing desired effects by bridging from what teachers know and can do to their potential to develop new skills and meet new challenges. Designing PD that aligns with teachers' zones of proximal development helps to ensure that the bridge endures (Vygotsky, 1978).

Table 3 Contrast of time 1 with time 2 of quality mathematics practice for intervention teachers

Domains and dimensions	Time 1 (n = 108)		Time 2 (n = 102)	
	M	SD	M	SD
What				
Learning objectives	4.06	1.52	4.32	1.18
Mathematical representations	4.13	1.47	4.24	1.20
Concept development	3.75	1.58	4.16	1.16
Who				
Attention to developmental trajectories	4.03	1.56	4.38	1.24
Response to individual students' needs	3.89	1.62	4.31	1.3
Developmental appropriate learning formats	3.81	1.60	4.14	1.31
How				
Planning	3.93	1.63	4.23	1.32
Student engagement	4.11	1.71	4.46	1.37
Establishment of math learning community	4.10	1.75	4.49	1.41

Online Resources for Symposia/Panel Discussion Sessions

Seminar on Symposium
http://www.slideshare.net/ShaellsJoshi/symposium-31123212
The author of this slide presentation describes the purpose, objective, features, scope, advantages and disadvantages of a symposium.

13 Guidelines for Great Panel Discussions
http://www.scottkirsner.com/panels.htm
Scott Kirsner provides advice for event organizers and moderators of panel discussions. He provides valuable information about logistics and technical issues that are sometimes overlooked.

How to Organize a Panel for a Conference
http://theprofessorisin.com/2013/03/15/how-to-organize-a-panel-for-a-conference/
Dr. Karen Kelsky's, former professor at the University of Oregon and the University of Illinois at Urbana-Champaign blog post provides information the steps one needs to take to organize a panel. It includes information on how junior professors should reach out to well established professors for guidance and participation.

Panel Discussion
http://www.nature.com/scitable/topicpage/panel-discussions-13909630
This site provides information about how to set up a panel discussion. It includes valuable information about the roles that moderators and panelists can play in managing the discussion.

Tips for Conference Discussants or Respondents
http://www.cgu.edu/PDFFiles/Writing%20Center/Writing%20Center%20Resources/Tips%20for%20Conf.%20Discussants%20and%20Respondents.pdf
This resource outlines the role of a discussant and includes suggestions for working effectively with discussants prior to and during a presentation.

Checklist for Symposia/Panel Discussion Sessions

Before the Symposium/Panel Session

- Print a copy of the session as described in the conference program and/or on the conference website. This will make it possible for you to identify and address the chair and other presenters by name when you introduce yourself.

- Prepare presentation materials at least two weeks ahead of time. This could include the paper itself, a one-page handout that summarizes the paper, a document that includes charts and tables that you hope to discuss with particpants, and/or a data collection instrument that you wish to share with attendees. In addition to the content include a cover page with the title of the paper, the date, your contact information and a QR code on the first slide. The QR code will make it possible for you attendees to access your material digitally and contact you later if they wish to reuse the material. Take at least 15 handouts.
- Save your presentation material and handouts on a flash drive and/or in the cloud if you use Google Drive or Dropbox so you can access your material if your laptop fails to function.
- Take business cards to share with attendees who might like to contact you later.
- Use the session number and title of the symposium to identify the room where you will present, locate the room, and check the set up in advance.

During the Symposium/Panel Session

- Reach the room at least 15 min before your session is scheduled to begin. Introduce yourself to the chair, and other presenters, if they are present. If not, you can start setting up the equipment. If a laptop has been provided you can transfer your presentation to the desktop of the laptop and encourage other presenters to do the same. This facilitates a smoother transition from one presentation to the next.
- Listen attentively to the chair's instructions about the protocol that will be followed. Some conferences require chairs to follow a pre-determined protocol, while others give chairs the freedom to decide how the session will be managed.
- Listen attentively to other presenters and take notes so you can contribute more meaningfully when the discussion ensues.
- Distribute your one-page handout to everyone just before you begin your presentation. Use it meaninfully and direct participants' attention to interesting trends and patterns in the data. Indicate very explictly the nature of the feedback you would like to receive.
- Introduce yourself, and then proceed with the presentation. Do not read the content included in your presentation material and/or handouts. Instead, use a conversational tone to describe the design of your study.
- Manage your presentation time appropriately either with the assistance of the chair or with a cell phone application that keeps time.
- Actively engage in the discussion with other presenters and attendees.
- Keep a record of all questions and comments from the audience members for future reference.

After the Symposium/Panel Session

- Approach attendees who showed a special interest in your topic and inquire about the work they have done in this area.

- Plan some time to debrief after the session and critique the presentation. If the session was successful, explore possibilities for presentations and publications that are collaborative.
- Thank the session chair personally at the end of the session, or later by email.
- Keep a record of all questions and comments from attendees for future reference.
- Correspond with fellow presenters who were particularly effective to explore other collaborative projects.

Chapter 9
Presenting from a Distance/Virtual Sessions

Given the ever-present need to cut costs, both for attendees, but also for conference organizers, distance/virtual sessions are gaining popularity. These sessions may be synchronous, with a designated time, or asynchronous, accessed at whatever time the conference participants wish. With synchronous sessions attendees typically see an image of the presenter and the visuals they have created on an LCD screen at the conference site. Attendees who are attending the conference virtually, from wherever they happen to be, can view the presentation on their computer screens. With asynchronous sessions the exchange takes place online during the predetermined timeframe.

Scope

Distance/virtual sessions have value for professionals at different stages of their careers. They provide presenters with an opportunity to describe new extensions to existing projects, newly initiated projects, and/or projects underway that include opportunities for additional partners. Technologies such as Picture Talk, WebEx, Gotomeetings, Zoom, Google hangout and a variety of other software applications are used to orchestrate virtual presentations which may take place in a synchronous or asynchronous format, as described below.

Format

A synchronous distance/virtual presentation could last anywhere between 30 and 90 min. In a synchronous format researcher, developers, and practitioners in different time zones and locations synchronously discuss, via web-based technology (e.g., Google hangout) their results and projects in progress with attendees. Presenters may be located in three different time zones, for example New York

M.R. Jalongo and C. Machado, *Making Effective Presentations at Professional Conferences*, SpringerBriefs in Education,
DOI 10.1007/978-3-319-23174-7_9

(10:00 a.m.), San Francisco (7:00 a.m.) and from the east in Europe, (4.00 p.m.). Depending upon how sophisticated the system is, attendees may be able to ask the presenter questions during the session, orally, or textually, using web-based technologies such as Twitter. Presenters can use the feedback to develop their idea, research questions, instrument, analytic approach etc. In an asynchronous format the discussion, related to condensed papers, takes place via the conference website and online discussion board. In addition to supporting an exchange of ideas the interaction facilitates networking between presenters and attendees.

How to Propose a Distance/Virtual Sessions

A distance/virtual proposal is approximately 2–3 paragraphs in length. Proposals generally include:

- a description of the problem and/or context,
- what they plan to show or demonstrate, and
- major aspects of the work and its importance. When appropriate they include relevant URLs and references.

Online Resources for Distance/Virtual Sessions

Virtual Presentations that Work
https://www.safaribooksonline.com/library/view/virtual-presentations-that/9780071739368/
In his book, sections of which are available online, Joel Gendelman provides readers with information about virtual presentations, the ways in which these can be used, and tips for troubleshooting.

Best Practices for Excellent Presentations in the Virtual World
https://cdns3.trainingindustry.com/media/3217793/mandel%20%20best%20practices%20for%20excellent%20virtual%20presentations.pdf
Produced by Mandel Communications, this resource provides readers with information about how to develop excellent webcast content and engage participants in a variety of ways.

Virtual Training: Are you Engaging or Boring?
http://www.learningsolutionsmag.com/articles/802/virtual-training-are-you-engaging-or-boring
In addition to general presentation skills, the author describes how the different features of conferencing software can be used to keep learners engaged.

Organizing a Teleconference
http://ctb.ku.edu/en/table-of-contents/structure/training-and-technical-assistance/design-training-session/main
This resource, maintained by The Community Toolbox, University of Kansas, provides information on how to design and deliver a teleconference, a checklist of planning considerations, and a PowerPoint that summarizes main information.

Virtual Presentations by Book Authors
http://www.edweb.net
Browse through this site and participate in some sessions to get oriented to professional development sessions on demand.

Checklist for a Distance/Virtual Sessions

Before the Distance/Virtual Session

- Prepare presentation material. In addition to the content include a cover page with the title of the session and your contact information on the first slide.
- Upload your brief paper and/or presentation material to the conference site several days before the due date.
- If you are using web-based technology to connect with a live audience at the conference collaborate with the on-site technical professionals affiliated with the conference to discuss how you can work together to make the session a success. Schedule a time to test the technology, including back up tools. Additionally, email the on-site professional a copy of visuals so they can be shared electronically if technology fails.

During the Distance/Virtual Session

The presentation skills that one acquires over a lifetime are often less relevant when one is presenting at a distance (Zelazny 2000).

- Make a conscious effort to mask the discomfort that comes with communication devoid of eye contact, instantaneous feedback and spontaneity.
- When leading an asynchronous session visit the site multiple times prior to and during the conference to interact with attendees.
- When leading a synchronous session locate yourself in a quiet space and be prepared to join the session at least 30 min ahead of time.

After the Distance/Virtual Presentation Session

- Follow up with attendees who showed a special interest in the session and inquire about the work they have done in this area. This interaction could lead to future partnerships.
- Record questions and responses from attendees for future reference.

Reference

Zelazny, G. (2000). *Say it with presentations: How to design and deliver successful business presentations*. New York, NY: McGraw-Hill.

Chapter 10
Keynote Address or Invited Session

A keynote address is a speech delivered by an invited guest at a large conference, and is often regarded as the jewel in the crown. Keynote speakers are selected on the basis of name recognition and are expected to bring the "wow" factor to a conference. They set the tone for the meeting, introduce the theme of the conference, rally the group to action, challenge attendees' thinking, and provide conference attendees with food for thought.

Scope

Depending upon the size and popularity of the conference, attendees of national and international conferences may have the opportunity to attend one or more keynote sessions. Inspirational speakers are generally chosen based on their exceptional public speaking skills and ability to intellectually stimulate an audience. They may be experts in the field or from very different fields; chosen to educate motivate, fuel change and growth, promote awareness, challenge the status quo, or present a fresh perspective. A photograph of each keynote speaker and/or invited speaker, the topic of their presentation, and brief biography is generally posted on the conference's webpage, often 6 months prior to the conference. These sessions are also advertised in the conference program. If you aspire to becoming a keynote speaker, do your "homework" by attending many keynote addresses and analyzing not only the message but also the delivery.

Format

A keynote address typically lasts approximately 45–60 min, followed by a brief question and answer session. This session is typically offered in one of the largest rooms at the conference site and can be attended by more than 500 people.

M.R. Jalongo and C. Machado, *Making Effective Presentations at Professional Conferences*, SpringerBriefs in Education,
DOI 10.1007/978-3-319-23174-7_10

A prominent member of the organization—often the president or the conference chairperson–introduces the speaker, highlighting his or her qualifications. Many times, this introduction describes how the keynote address fits into or expands the overall conference theme. This helps the attendees to form a global view of both the keynote session and the conference as a whole. Introductions highlight the nature of the contribution that the speaker has made to the discipline or content area. The speaker then takes the floor and presents for about 45–60 min. Following this, the speaker may or may not respond to questions or present at other, smaller sessions.

How to Select a Keynote Speaker

Beginning and mid-career faculty who are invited to serve on a conference committee may be required to help identify keynote speakers. Some conferences employ a peer-nomination process, and accept self-nominations. Others require conference committees to use clearly defined selection criteria which may include all or some of the following:

- Well respected in the field, for their scholarship, service and/or teaching.
- Have published a widely read book or body of research on a topic of interest to the audience.
- Have presented to an audience of a similar size.
- Have expertise in a content area that relates to the conference theme.
- Can bring a new perspective.
- Have not presented a keynote at the conference for a designated window of time, which is often a period of 2–5 years.

At major conferences, keynote speakers typically are offered both expenses, which include reimbursement for travel, lodging and food, and an honorarium. The conference committee should discuss, in advance, their expectations of the keynote speaker. This could include the expectation that the keynote speaker mingle with the participants for a day, serve on a panel, have a meal with the conference committee and/or offer one or more sessions in addition to delivering the keynote address.

How to Plan a Keynote or Invited Speaker Address

A keynote is both similar and different from other conference presentations. Like other conference presentations, it is as much about substance as it is about style; it cannot be improvised. Effective public speakers begin with momentum, speak with energy, and use a conversational tone with their audience "rather than reading to them or just dumping content on them" (Chesebro 2014, p. 251). Box 10.1 presents examples of inspiring keynote speeches.

Box 10.1 Sources for Keynote Addresses

Vital Speeches of the Day—This publication includes the script for outstanding speeches delivered by effective public speakers, across disciplines.

Professional Organizations—Many professional groups videotape outstanding speeches or publish the papers on which a particularly effective speech was based. Check the catalogs of your professional groups and the journals for examples.

TED Talks—Watch videos such as "The Secret Structure of Great Talks" (ted.com), How to Give a TED Talk (YouTube), "How to Deliver the Talk of Your Life" (sixminutes.dlugan.com/how-to-deliver-talk-life)

To communicate the message clearly keynote speakers have to pick out important information, organize it, and connect it to existing knowledge. Verderber et al. (2014) emphasize the importance of "effective research" and "audience analysis and adaptation." They also recommend that presenters employ a recursive rather than linear approach during the development stage; this allows the presenter to go back and forth between steps. For example, the initial topic might change significantly after the presenter does some preliminary research or analysis of audience.

Presentation material should complement rather than replace the presenter. Preparing a speech is different from preparing a written document. The visual material that the speaker creates will help to keep them on track. A keynote address that is packed with too much information could result in cognitive overload. Chesebro (2014) advises presenters to confine themselves to 2–3 points, presented on less than five slides with no more than seven words on each line. Additionally, they are advised to make the relationship between ideas more obvious.

Platow (2002) recommends the use of rhetorical questions which have the potential to stimulate thinking, but only if the questions relate to a strong argument. Humor helps to make content memorable and makes it easier for attendees to relate to terms that are applied to technical issues. Presenters should consider scrutinizing the content of the presentation to determine where humor should be injected. A "word, a phrase, or a box in the theoretical model can be altered with something humorous that will lighten the material a bit and emphasize a particular concept" (Berk 2003, p. 154). Humor should not derail the train of thought. Presenters should retain a pool of backup humorous material that can be substituted at the last minute, especially if previous suggestions indicate that the ones already in the speech will not work (Berk 2003). Platow (2002) recommends that presenters who are not funny should use humor, but only after receiving honest feedback from a colleague.

Platow (2002) emphasizes the importance of *correct impression management*. Poorly prepared presenters who come across as "boring, aloof, nervous, or incompetent" (p. 3) lose the attention of audiences not just at that session but at sessions in the future. Practicing a speech multiple times will help the presenter to come across as "natural, spontaneous, effortless, and authoritative" (Berk 2003,

p. 157). Russell and Munter (2011) indicate that if this is done in front of a mirror or video recorded then presenters will have the opportunity to analyze their nonverbal communication and address distracting habits.

Activity: Evaluating a TED Talk

The TED conference series has been offering enlightening talks for 30 years. Presenters can learn a great deal about public speaking by listening to great speakers, and evaluating the techniques they employ. Following text analysis of a professional presentation Movshovitz-Hadar and Hazzan (2004) identified six best practices of a strong presentation. Use the checklist in Box 10.2 which is based on their work, to evaluate a TED talk of your choice, available at http://www.ted.com. One particularly good speech is from Sir Ken Robinson, "Do Schools Kill Creativity?"

Box. 10.2 Checklist for Evaluating a Speech

- Did the speaker begin with a structural overview (or mental map) of the talk?
- Set the listeners at ease?
- Fill in the details?
- Supply concrete examples to illustrate key concepts?
- Embed the explanation of concepts within the presentation?
- Relate details back to the original mental map to orient listeners?
- Restate the thesis at the end with a succinct summary?

Online Resources for a Keynote or Invited Sessions

World Class Keynote Speakers
http://www.globalchange.com/keynotespeakers.htm
Dr. Patrick Dixon, often described as Europe's leading futurist, identifies the skills of a world class keynote speaker. Additionally, he lists ways to assess a keynote speaker prior to an assignment, and common mistakes to avoid.

Keynote Speaker: How to Develop an Impactful Keynote Presentation
http://www.sellingergroup.com/keynote-speaker-how-to-deliver-a-keynote-speech.html

This webpage includes links to 11 video clips produced by the Sellinger Group. The presenter delivers information about topics like keynote layout strategies, proof tools, and presentation sequence.

How to Create and Deliver an Effective Keynote Speech
http://www.quickanddirtytips.com/business-career/public-speaking/how-to-create-and-deliver-an-effective-keynote-speech
Lisa B. Marshall of The Public Speaker describes aspects that makes a keynote speech different from other speeches.

13 Tips for Delivering a Memorable Keynote Speech
http://smallbiztrends.com/2013/03/13-public-speaking-tips.html
The author of this article summarizes the comments made by promising young entrepreneurs of the Young Entrepreneur Council (YEC) in response to the question: "What is your best tip for writing a great, memorable keynote-type speech that genuinely inspires the audience?"

Checklist for Keynote Address or Invited Session

Before Agreeing to Deliver the Keynote Address/Conduct an Invited Sessions

- Reflect on the theme of the conference, often announced several months before the conference, and create a list of potential topics that align with the theme of the conference.
- Schedule a telephone conversation with conference organizers to gain insight into their expectations. Thank them for the invitation. Be upfront about your expectations in terms of fees, travel expenses, and the level of interaction you will have with attendees.
- Share the potential list of topics you have identified with conference organizers. Finalize the topic of your presentation and notify them officially in writing.

Before the Keynote/Invited Speaker Session

- Study the conference website, call for proposals, and the titles of other invited guests to learn more about your audience prior to writing your speech.
- Write your speech and develop supporting presentation material well in advance. You should begin working on a keynote as soon as you receive the invitation; do not procrastinate. Many times, you will be asked to supply a recent photograph, a description for inclusion in the program, and a short synopsis of your professional credentials. Slides should include a cover page with the title of the paper, the date, your contact information and a QR code on the first slide. The QR code will make it possible for you attendees to access your material digitally and contact you later.
- Rehearse your speech—both the content and delivery—and seek oral and written peer-critique.

- Print a copy of the session as described in the conference program and/or on the conference website so you can identify and address the chair and conference organizers appropriately.
- Prepare for equipment malfunction. Save your presentation material and handouts on a flash drive and/or in the cloud if you use Google Drive or Dropbox. E-mail a copy to yourself.
- Take business cards to share with attendees who might like to contact you later.
- Visit the room where you will present prior to the session and double-check the sound, projection, and schedule.
- Let the conference planners know as soon as you arrive on site. Arrive at the room at least 15 min before your session is scheduled to begin. Introduce yourself to the chair, and other conference organizers.
- Seek assistance in displaying your presentation material on the projector.

During the Keynote/Invited Speaker Session

- Listen attentively to the chair's remarks about you and respond graciously before you begin your speech. Thank the participants for attending.
- Let your personality show as you deliver your speech.
- Manage presentation time appropriately either with the assistance of the chair or with a cell phone application that keeps time.
- Respond thoughtfully to questions and comments.

After the Keynote/Invited Speaker Session

- Mingle informally with conference organizers, the session chair, and attendees as they prepare to leave. Give them your business card, if requested.
- Thank the conference organizers in person and follow up with a thank you card immediately after the conference.
- Keep a record of all questions and comments from attendees for future reference.

References

Berk, R. A. (2003). *Professors are from mars, students are from snickers: how to write and deliver humor in the classroom and in professional presentations*. Sterling, VA: Stylus.

Cheseboro, J. L. (2014). *Professional communication at work: Interpersonal strategies for Career Success*. CN: Greenwood Press.

Movshovitz-Hadar, N., & Hazzan, O. (2004). How to present it? On the rhetoric of an outstanding lecturer. *International Journal of Mathematical Education in Science and Technology, 35*(6), 813–827.

Platow, M. (2002). *Giving professional presentations in the behavioral sciences and related fields*. New York, NY: Psychology Press.

Verderber, R., Sellnow, D., & Verderber, K. (2014). *The challenge of effective speaking in a digital age*. Boston, MA: Cengage Learning.

Part III
After the Conference

Chapter 11
From Presentations to Publications

When three professors offered a session at a conference called "From a Conference Presentation to Publication" it was very well attended. Many of the participants indicated that, although they presented regularly at conferences, they had not produced a written manuscript on those topics. Evidently, this group was not atypical. Research indicates that a small percentage of scholars from various fields who present at conferences generate a peer-reviewed journal article from that work, even when they presented a paper at the conference (Joubert and Cronje 2003). In a study by Richling et al. (2014), just 8–10 % of presenters at a major conference went on to publish a manuscript. This is unfortunate for many reasons. First of all, it fails to support professionals in "working smarter" and maximizing scholarly productivity goals. Secondly, it deprives professionals who could not attend the conference session from learning what these scholars had to offer. Third, many journal editors bemoan the fact that much of what is submitted for publication is not suitable for their readership. Effective presenters have the advantage of already "field testing" their work with an audience of peers (Levin 2012).

Advantages of Beginning with a Conference Presentation

Using a successful presentation as the basis for a professional publication has much to recommend it (Happell 2008). For example:

- Momentum to continue with the work has been established
- Material is already structured in a logical way
- Content is audience-centered
- Peers have already reviewed and responded to the work
- The manuscript is an extension and elaboration of previously completed work
- Ideas have been enriched and enlarged by the questions and comments of an audience
- The material is peppered with examples that make written work more interesting

M.R. Jalongo and C. Machado, *Making Effective Presentations at Professional Conferences*, SpringerBriefs in Education,
DOI 10.1007/978-3-319-23174-7_11

To illustrate how conference sessions can lead to scholarly writing, consider how one faculty member generated various projects from the same basic body of work. First, she made a presentation at a local conference that was well received. Next, she wrote an article for the national newsletter of an organization and produced a brochure for families published by the National Parent Teacher Association. After that, she published a review of the literature based on the preparation done for a national conference presentation. Then she wrote two practical articles on the topic and finally, proposed a book that was published by the leading professional association in her field.

Activity: Multiple Scholarly Spin-Offs

Draw a circle and put the topic of a successful conference presentation in the center. Now make a web or map of related scholarly projects that could be generated from that experience. Remember to think in terms of different audiences, a more specific focus, and different formats.

Different Types of Writing Tasks

Conference presenters are called upon to produce different types of writing that can serve as a resource when writing for publication. Some typical writing tasks include the abstract, a poster, a proposal, a brief paper distributed at the session, or a complete paper published as conference proceedings. Each of these is discussed below.

Abstracts

Often an abstract determines whether or not the session will be accepted and is the only thing that the conference planners publish, so this piece of writing is important. Both for practical articles and research articles, a well-written conference abstract can become the basis for the article abstract. Some advantages of beginning with a conference abstract are:

- If the proposal was peer-reviewed, the abstract was already earned the acceptance of professional peers
- Writing the abstract distils the work to its very essence and can suggest the main headings of a published paper

- If a well-attended and well-received conference session resulted from the abstract published in the conference program, it suggests that peers found it interesting and that it effectively conveyed the purpose
- If the abstract was written to mesh with a particular conference theme, the organization may be more keen to publish on that topic
- Having a well written abstract is a helpful starting point for a journal article or book chapter. In many cases, it can be modified slightly and used again in a written manuscript that requires an abstract.

Posters

Posters often report on a work in progress and may include an accompanying, short paper that can be distributed on site. The advantage of a poster as a starting point for a publishable article is that an effective poster is clear, concise, and informative. The presenter often is required to include an abstract, conclusion, visual data, references, and contact information—all items that will be useful when composing an article or book chapter. In addition, preparing a poster requires presenters to anticipate questions and, if they take notes on the feedback from visitors to their posters, this can strengthen the overall presentation of written work. In many ways, a high-quality poster is a roadmap for a professional journal article, book chapter, or converting a dissertation into a publication In addition, if the presenter was required to produce a short paper, it can be elaborated into a full-length report of the research.

Conference Proposals

Major conferences often require a proposal that is 2–5 pages in length; some of the highly respected professional organizations also send these proposals out for peer review. Thus, when the conference proposal is accepted, it is a form of validation for the work. Knowing that fellow professionals with no vested interest in the proposer's success have given the project a positive evaluation should build self-confidence about pursuing publication. This vote of confidence extends, not only to research but also to workshop/training types of presentations. In preparing the proposal, scholars often are required to identify benefits for the participants and beginning a practical article with this audience-centered perspective represents a distinct advantage. Conference selection committees generally are seeking innovation in what is presented and expect conference presenters to make the nature of the contribution clear. Starting with this firmly in mind is an avenue to preparing a better professional journal article, book chapter, or book.

Different categories of sessions (see Chaps. 4–10) also yield different types of publications. If, for example, a distinguished panel of presenters makes a presentation on a timely topic, this can become the basis for a "question and answer" type of practical article with the various speakers weighing in on each issue or perhaps an edited book with each presenter submitting one of the chapters. Likewise, all day or multiple day presentations can form the foundation for a book proposal, such as a college-level textbook or a scholarly book.

Conference Papers

Conferences also offer opportunities to publish short papers and full-length manuscripts, at least as conference proceedings (Daniels 2013). Some different types of papers include:

- Developmental papers that report ongoing research and allow researchers to gain feedback during their research process
- Short papers that are shared with attendees during the session
- Full reports of completed research in a format suitable for publication

Some conferences require papers from the presenters and then publish only the best as conference proceedings. This often requires peer review and revisions prior to acceptance (Rowley 2012).

Ordinarily, the fact that a manuscript was published as conference proceedings does not prohibit the author from pursuing formal publication in a peer-reviewed journal—unless the conference proceedings are copyrighted. That is why, when reading published articles, you often will see an acknowledgement that the work was shared at a conference previously. The same guidelines hold true for Education Resources Information Center (ERIC); even though the presenters may be contacted after a major conference and invited to submit their conference papers for dissemination, this is not a "real" publication and the author retains copyright. Universities differ in how they evaluate conference proceedings as scholarly work, so be certain to determine the value of works disseminated in this way prior to investing a huge effort in a paper published as conference proceedings.

Consider drafting a paper even if a conference does not require it (Happell 2009). This advice pertains to a wide range of presentation types, whether it is a poster session, a workshop/training, a research forum, panel presentation, or keynote address. The paper can serve as a guide during the presentation while the comments made and questions raised during the discussion can suggest revisions that would improve the work. Revisit the draft paper while enthusiasm for the project is still high and make the most of otherwise wasted time—for example, reread it while waiting at the airport or make some revisions during the flight home. Written papers also are a good way to mentor students or less experienced colleagues. One professor and an undergraduate student used a "reverse outline" technique (Garaffa and Brians 2011). They generated the paper first and then pulled out talking points for use during the presentation. Collaborating in this way lessened fears and worries for the student who was presenting for the first time because this approach not only provided ample opportunity for revision and proofreading but also made both of them knowledgeable about the entire project and confident in their preparation.

Caveats When Transitioning from Oral to Written Work

Even though the advantages of beginning with a successful conference presentation are numerous, there are some important differences between oral and written presentations. Issues to consider are:

- When writing it is more difficult to convey affective qualities (e.g., the presenter's enthusiasm) that are evident in a face-to-face presentation
- Presentations often include anecdotes that are difficult to "translate" into concise written examples
- Presentations are sometimes on popular topics that are already well represented in professional publications, so publishing will demand a fresh perspective on the topic
- Presentations are sometimes fairly generic whereas writing tends to require a sharper focus on a particular facet of the topic so that it can be treated thoroughly in a short manuscript
- Those who review a written manuscript may be less interested in and informed about the topic than participants at a conference
- The structure of an oral presentation may be more predictable (e.g., chronological) while a written work may require a very different type of organization in order to sustain readers' interest
- The style of written work often is more formal than that expected during an oral presentation at a conference, so the author will need to adjust accordingly.

Strategies for Generating a Manuscript

You'll also want to think about the process that you can use to make the draft paper more publishable. Some suggestions on getting started are:

- *Identify suitable outlets.* Calls for papers often are distributed at the conference; check the bulletin boards, display tables, and electronic media. Professional associations frequently have a book publication program in addition to a journal and they may be seeking book authors or chapters for an edited book. Attend the open meetings or sessions on writing for publication to learn more about upcoming projects, the proposal process, and so forth. Some professional associations publish brochures on timely topics, monographs, single-authored books, and edited books; they may also have guest editors for their journals.

- *Maximize networking*. Prospective co-authors, editors, and publishers can be identified while attending the conference. The American Educational Research Association (AERA), for example, sponsors Journal Talks—roundtable discussions with editors of journals. This gives attendees an opportunity to discuss their ideas for a publication with an editor, face-to-face. Sometimes, an editor or publisher is favorably impressed by your presentation and will share a business card. Be sure to follow up with such invitations by submitting a carefully crafted manuscript that adheres to the journal's guidelines.
- *Revisit the work.* Try to capture the passion that you have for your topic in the new medium. Think about the examples that worked well and review the questions that were asked. If you weren't entirely satisfied with your answers, identify recent and authoritative sources of support and develop a better response. Look over the evaluations to gain some insight. Sometimes, one particular part of what you shared will generate the most positive feedback and this could become a focus for a publication.
- *Check and double check.* Make certain that documentation is complete and accurate. Study the publisher's guidelines carefully. While some minor formatting mistakes might be tolerated during an oral presentation, adherence to publication guidelines and the citation style required by a scholarly publisher is essential.. Remember that only the works actually cited are listed in the references rather than everything that was read.

Acquiring Skill as a Reviewer

Yet another way to build skill in writing for publication is to serve as a volunteer reviewer for conference proposals. Usually, it is easier to detect the weaknesses in someone else's written work than in our own writing. Large, highly competitive conferences may use an anonymous peer review system to select proposals while smaller conferences or a special interest groups (SIG) within a larger conference may use a selection committee. Look into the leading organizations in your field and volunteer for this type of service. The group typically will provide you with a scoring sheet and working with these criteria helps reviewers to internalize the elements of a successful proposal (Tappe and Galer-Unti 2009). Frequently, the "bottom line" question is: Would *I* want to be in the audience for this session or, if not, would I recommend it to colleagues with this area of interest? Similar questions apply to manuscripts for journal articles, book chapters and scholarly books, namely: Do I wish that I had written this? Would I recommend that it be published so that others have access to it?

Some general evaluation criteria for conference proposals that are equally applicable to journal articles, book chapters, and books are:

- Does the work conform to the guidelines? Too often, conference proposals and other types of manuscripts are prepared in haste and rejected without review because the authors failed to follow the rules.
- Is the work appropriate for the audience? There should be a clear match between the manuscript and the intended audience, both for conference proposals and other types of academic writing.
- Does the work represent effective scholarly writing? Manuscripts that are not well written are routinely rejected. Awkwardly worded sentences, disorganized thinking, and careless mistakes are sufficient justification for rejection, even if the quality of the thinking is good.
- Does the work hold promise for advancing thinking in the field? The writer needs to move the audience beyond what is already widely known and readily available from existing sources.

For more detailed advice on reviewing conference proposals, (see Bussema and Nemec 2007) and Reviewing Conference Papers (www.markbernstein.org/elements/Reviewing.pdf)

Conclusion

As this chapter has described, the thick programs that are distributed at major conferences suggest that many scholars are active in making presentations while far fewer take the next step and transform an oral presentation into a written and publishable piece. When we talk with faculty and students about writing for publication, one of the most common questions has to do with how to generate more than one scholarly product from the same basic body of work. One recommended way of doing this is to convert effective oral presentations at conferences into written publications. Doing this seldom runs the risk of repeating the same work—as another conference presentation on the same topic would—because oral communication is so different from written language. Tenure and evaluation committees typically understand that sharing work in an entirely different format with a specific audience and focus renews, rather than merely replicates, the work. Therefore, mastering the process of converting a successful conference presentation into an article, book chapter, or book is a key to increasing scholarly productivity in a highly efficient manner.

Online Writing Resources for Presenters

Guide to American Psychological Association Style
https://owl.english.purdue.edu/owl/section/2/10/
The Purdue OWL offers a "crash course" on American Psychological Association (APA) Style as well as many resources on writing more effectively that are YouTube vidcasts.

Tierney, T. S., & Lozano, A. M. (2011). Presentation to publication. *Journal of Neurosurgery, 115*(6), 1256–1257.

Two physicians provide helpful tips on making the transition from an oral presentation to a published paper.

Preparing for Conference Presentations

http://sterneworks.org/delgado.html

Sage advice for graduate students on conference papers from conference planner Fernando Delgado.

From Conference Presentation to publication: What is Happening to Australia's Palliative Literature?

http://www.caresearch.com.au/Caresearch/Portals/0/Documents/ABOUT-CARESEARCH/Project-Resources/FromConferencePrestationtoPublication.pdf

This exemplary research poster from Tieman and Currow (2003) reports on the conversion rates of presentations into publications for professionals in the medical field. Only about 16 % of presenters generated published work based on their conference presentations.

References

Bussema, E., & Nemec, P. (2007). Conference presentations. *Psychiatric Rehabilitation Journal, 30*(3), 231–233.

Daniels, G. (2013). How to get your abstract accepted and how to present it. *ISBT Science Series, 9* (1), 51–55. doi:10.1111/voxs.12069.

Garaffa, T., & Brians, C. L. (2011). Two views of a conference presentation: An undergraduate's first research conference experience. *Journal of Political Science Education, 7*(2), 240–242. doi:10.1080/15512169.2011.564910.

Happell, B. (2009). Presenting with precision: Preparing and delivering a polished conference presentation. *Nurse Researcher, 16*(3), 45–56.

Happell, B. (2008). From conference presentation to publication: A guide. *Nurse Researcher, 15* (2), 40–48.

Joubert, G., & Cronje, H. S. (2003). From a research presentation to a publication. *SAMJ, 94*(12), 965–966. Retrieved June 8, 2015 from http://www.samj.org.za/index.php/samj/article/viewFile/2825/2026.

Levin, B. (2012). Why don't we learn at education conferences? *Phi Delta Kappan, 94*(3), 74–75.

Richling, S. M., Rapp, J. T., Funk, J. A.., D'Agostini, J., Garrido, N., & Moreno, V. (2014). Low publication rate of 2005 conference presentations: Implications for practitioners serving individuals with autism and intellectual disabilities. *Research in Developmental Disabilities, 35* (11), 2744–2751.

Rowley, J. (2012). Six steps to successful academic conference presentations. *Marketing Review, 12*(4), 437–450. doi:10.1362/146934712X13546196910891.

Tappe, M. K., & Galer-Unti, R. A. (2009). Health educators' role in promoting health literacy and advocacy for the 21st century. *Journal of School Health, 71*(10), 477–478. doi:10.1111/j.1746-1561.2001.tb07284.

Kolibri 360 GmbH
Ferdinand-Jühlke-Straße 7
99095 Erfurt, Deutschland
produktsicherheit@kolibri360.de